LIGHT IN A DARK PLACE

Also by Henry Gariepy

Names and Titles of Jesus
1974

Footsteps to Calvary
1977

Study Guide –
Footsteps to Calvary
1977

The Advent of Jesus Christ
1979

Study Guide –
The Advent of Jesus Christ
1979

100 Portraits of Christ
1987

Portraits of Perseverance
1989

Christianity in Action
1990

Wisdom to Live By
1991

General of God's Army
1993

Challenge and Response
1994

40 Days with the Savior
1995

LIGHT IN A DARK PLACE

HENRY GARIEPY

VICTOR BOOKS
A DIVISION OF SCRIPTURE PRESS PUBLICATIONS INC.
USA CANADA ENGLAND

Copyediting: Barbara Williams
Cover Design: Grace K. Chan Mallette
Cover Photo: FPG International Corp.

Library of Congress Cataloging-in-Publication Data

Gariepy, Henry.
Light in a dark place / by Henry Gariepy.
p. cm.
ISBN 1-56476-452-4
1. Bible. O.T. Prophets—Commentaries. I. Title.
BS1505.3.G37 1995
224'.07—dc20 95-3969
CIP

---

1 2 3 4 5 6 7 8 9 10 Printing/Year 99 98 97 96 95

DEDICATION

To Stephen and Susan
Son and Daughter-in-love
Who are living out the message of this book.

THE AUTHOR

Henry Gariepy is a Colonel and National Literary Secretary and Editor in Chief for The Salvation Army, with his office and home in Alexandria, Virginia. He is a prolific writer of books and articles. Two of his twelve books have exceeded 150,000 copies with some going into multiple editions and translations abroad.

His authorized biography of General Eva Burrows has a foreword by Billy Graham and has had a distribution in over 100 countries.

The author maintains an active schedule of speaking engagements, including Bible conferences and national writers conferences. He earned his Bachelor of Arts and Master of Science degrees at Cleveland State University. He is an outdoor enthusiast, including being a three-time twenty-six mile marathon finisher. He and his wife Marjorie take great delight in their four children and eleven grandchildren.

Contents

Foreword

THOSE OF US WHOSE DELIGHT in literary excursions into the world of Scripture has been wonderfully enhanced by the guidance of Henry Gariepy await with eagerness each new collection of his devotional meditations. And we are never disappointed. In *Light in a Dark Place,* Colonel Gariepy discovers amidst the sometimes puzzling and obscure texts of the Old Testament prophets a lively, human dimension that speaks tellingly to our time.

Peering into the future, the prophets wrote as they were borne along by the Holy Spirit. They were very much in touch with the mind of God. But they were also immersed in the day-to-day realities that make up our own experience. Henry Gariepy has a remarkable gift for drawing attention to the radiant relevance of the truth they recorded for the nitty-gritty issues of Christian obedience in every age. He employs that gift again with the same skillful use of language that has been his hallmark over the years. He draws upon a lifetime of disciplined study of the Word of God, his own extensive reading, and long experience in engaging the toughest challenges of our society.

Colonel Gariepy has had a distinguished career as a Salvation Army officer. He has won the admiration of his peers in the trenches of combat with the causes of human suffering. As a writer and long-time Editor-in-Chief of National Publications for The Salvation Army in the United States of America, he has exerted a gracious influence that has ranged far beyond his own denominational moorings. Again, he leaves us in his debt with gratitude for the manner in which he has shared so freely and helpfully with us all.

May the Spirit of Light and Truth use these meditations to aid us all in penetrating the dark, suffocating moral confusion of our day with the light of the knowledge of the glory of God in the face of Jesus revealed in His prophetic Word.

Visit then this soul of mine,
Pierce the gloom of sin and grief;
Fill me, Radiance divine,
Scatter all my unbelief;
More and more thyself display,
Shining to the perfect day.

General Paul A. Rader
International Leader of The Salvation Army
London, England

Introduction

PROPHETIC WRITINGS COMPRISE over one half of the Bible and contain some of the most vital teachings and truths of Scripture. The New Testament emphasizes the critical importance of prophecy: *And we have the word of the prophets made more certain, and you will do well to pay attention to it, as to a light shining in a dark place, until the day dawns and the morning star rises in your hearts. . . . For prophecy never had its origin in the will of man, but men spoke from God as they were carried along by the Holy Spirit* (2 Peter 1:19, 21).

Jesus Himself, in His post-resurrection appearance to the two disciples on the Emmaus Road, chided His followers for not giving proper attention to the prophetic writings: *How foolish you are, and how slow of heart to believe all that the prophets have spoken! . . . And beginning with Moses and all the prophets, He explained to them what was said in all the Scriptures concerning Himself* (Luke 24:25, 27).

Thus the prophetic writings of the Bible are worthy of our most careful and prayerful study. These seventeen Old Testament books are indeed "as a light shining in a dark place." Their luminous truths serve as guideposts for the difficult and often dangerous paths of life we are called to journey.

The books of the prophets are generally not as well known as other parts of the Bible, often because they pose difficult reading and understanding. Beautiful pearls of insight and inspiration, loose and unstrung, lie tucked away in these ancient books of the Bible. This writing seeks to bring together some of these pearls from the prophets into a necklace of devotional truths to enrich the lives of God's people.

Isaiah will speak to us with his immortal words on the advent and mission of our Lord. Some lesser known but priceless pearls are harvested from the depths of this book, such as the eloquent expression of our Lord's love, *See, I have engraved you on the palms of My hands* (49:16). Those going through dark valleys will find comfort in the precious promise: *I will give you the treasures of darkness, riches stored in secret places* (45:3). The resolution of the Messiah in His mission of sacrifice is reflected in the pearl, *Therefore have I set My face like a flint* (50:7). And here in this "Gospel According to Isaiah," Christ is portrayed as the bloodstained but triumphant warrior in the metaphorical text: *I have trodden the winepress alone* (63:3).

In Jeremiah, the longest book in the Bible in content, we see represented the prophet's awesome awareness of God. Ezekiel speaks to us of the holiness of God. From the startling stories and sublime visions of Daniel we see life and history in the perspective of God's eternal purpose.

Hosea, in the second greatest love story in the Bible, portrays for us the costliness of forgiveness. The love story of Hosea is the spiritual biography of every person as he reveals to us the greatest wonder of the universe—the divine pursuit of the love of God for lost sinners.

Joel flings out the pearl of promise of the outpouring of the Holy Spirit. The thunder of God's wrath reverberates from the pages of the peasant Amos, who enlarges our concept of sin as it relates to economic oppression and injustice. The story of Jonah finds an echo in the failure of our own hearts as we are reminded that we serve the God of the second chance. Micah, another son of the soil who went from plowman to God's penman, is a prophet with a mighty message that culminates in some of the most extraordinary and best known texts of the Bible. The winds of war blow through the Book of Nahum, but he tells of the God who is a refuge in the storms of violence. The towering truth of Habakkuk's "living by faith" became a landmark of New Testament theology and church history.

These and other treasured truths and timeless themes make up a spiritual necklace of priceless pearls from the prophets that can enrich and enhance our lives. Let us enter prayerfully upon our journey with the prophets.

I S A I A H

PRINCE OF THE PROPHETS

1

PRINCE OF THE PROPHETS

ISAIAH STANDS FOREMOST among the celebrated prophets of the Old Testament. He towers without peer for his unsurpassed poetry and distinguished statesmanship. The book's prominence among the Dead Sea Scrolls and quotes from it by the first-century Jewish historian Josephus further witness to its popularity.

Isaiah has parallels to the Bible as a whole. The Bible has sixty-six books; Isaiah sixty-six chapters. The Old Testament has thirty-nine books. The first division of Isaiah has thirty-nine chapters. The New Testament has twenty-seven books, the last section of Isaiah twenty-seven chapters. The Old Testament deals with Israel's sin and God's judgment, as does the first section of Isaiah. The New Testament presents the mission of Christ, as do the last twenty-seven chapters of Isaiah.

Isaiah is the most quoted Old Testament book in the New Testament. It is quoted or alluded to 472 times in twenty-three of the New Testament's twenty-seven books.

The prophet's poetic passages are marked by majesty and beauty of expression, brilliant word pictures, and polished literary art. He had the largest vocabulary of Old Testament writers, using nearly 2,200 different Hebrew words. He is also credited with writing a history of the reign of King Uzziah (2 Chron. 26:22).

Isaiah lived and worked in Jerusalem during the stormy period from about 750 to 700 B.C., a time of international turbulence, political chaos, and moral breakdown. The Assyrian war machine was on a roll and Israel was in its path. A second-century Jewish writing, "The Martyrdom of Isaiah," helped form the tradition that Isaiah was martyred, believed to have been "sawn in two" (Heb. 11:37) during the reign of Hezekiah's evil son, Manasseh (2 Kings 21:16).

The Unity of Isaiah

How many Isaiahs were there? Like Manasseh, scholars have sawed this writer into two authors based on the major difference in theme and writing from chapter 40 on.

Such fragmentation is not supported by the Isaiah Scroll found in the Qumran caves near the Dead Sea, and thought to have been copied about 100 B.C. This oldest Hebrew text of Isaiah, a leather scroll now in Jerusalem, shows no break between chapters 39 and 40. There is no manuscript or traditional support for the theory of dual authorship.

Isaiah's special title for God, "Holy One of Israel," is prominent in both sections of his book, occurring twelve times in chapters 1–39 and fourteen times in 40–46, but found only six times in the rest of the Old Testament. Twenty-five other Hebrew words or expressions are found in both divisions of the book that do not occur in any other prophetic writing. Chapters 36–39 present a historical interlude and introduction to chapters 40–66, providing a structural unity. The second-century Septuagint translation gives no indication of dual authorship. Furthermore, it is not plausible that such a peerless writer would disappear from the scene of history.

The New Testament quotes from both sections of Isaiah as one author: Matthew 12:17-21 (Isa. 42:1-4); Matthew 3:3 and Luke 3:4 (Isa. 40:3); Romans 10:16, 20 (Isa. 53:1; 65:1); John 12:38-41 (Isa. 53:1; 6:10).

Themes and Theology

The thunder of God's judgment can be heard rumbling through these chapters. But the divine call to salvation also sounds loud and clear. The Messiah lives within its pages, with more messianic prophecies in the Book of Isaiah than all the other prophets combined. The Suffering Servant, the One "wounded for our transgressions" and "bruised for our iniquities" is portrayed in immortal words. The prophet, in his sublime fifty-third chapter, takes us to the foot of the cross in his portrayal of the Suffering Savior. This prince of the prophets also lifts our thoughts to lofty heights of the sovereign God, "the everlasting God, the Creator of the ends of the earth" (Isa. 40:28).

Isaiah is the book of golden texts that through the centuries continue to enrich the life of the believer. When venturing on a journey through Isaiah, we should come with great expectations. It is the book of the true "New Age"—God's new age of peace and righteousness.

Lord, as we commence this study of Your Word through the prophets of old, our hearts echo the longing of the psalmist, "Open my eyes that I may see wonderful things in Your Law" (Ps. 119:18).

2

Isaiah Speaks to Our Day

Read Isaiah 1

Isaiah, prince of the prophets, launches his magnificent manuscript with his byline, commission, and the historical context of the book, all in the opening verse: *The vision concerning Judah and Jerusalem that Isaiah son of Amoz saw during the reigns of Uzziah, Jotham, Ahaz and Hezekiah, kings of Judah.* The prophet is not speaking his own words, but proclaiming the revelation from God.

Rebellion against God

Throughout the book, the phrase *The Lord has spoken* (1:2) introduces God as principal speaker. The opening scene is as a courtroom. The heavens are called as witnesses. Israel is the accused. The plaintiff is God Himself. The charge: rebellion. In a blistering indictment God charges: *They have rebelled against Me.* Isaiah preaches the hard truth that the nation has *forsaken the Lord; they have spurned the Holy One of Israel and turned their backs on Him* (v. 4). The word "rebelled" is apt for Isaiah's parent-child analogy.

God is speaking to Israel as a father: *I reared children and brought them up* (v. 2). Disappointment marks His message to them. Employing striking imagery, the prophet quotes God as saying that, unlike Israel, even domestic animals know their master (v. 3). They are accused of forgetting and forsaking God. Total devastation will be the sentence for the apostate nation (vv. 5-8).

"Some survivors" (v. 9) becomes the first intimation of "the remnant" that will recur as a major theme of this book. God's ultimate purpose for the redemption of man will not be aborted. There will be those, albeit a small number, who will be faithful and will know His blessings in the age to come.

The Lord through Isaiah denounces the people's hollow sacrificial systems that are poor substitutes for righteousness (vv. 10-15). There can be no gap between our worship and our living. Let us beware that we do not offer empty rituals in place of the moral purity and true worship God requires.

A Compelling Invitation

In the midst of this dark picture of rebellion and judgment, a note of hope is sounded. God calls His children to repentance: *Wash and make yourselves clean. Take your evil deeds out of My sight! Stop doing wrong, learn to do right!* God calls the nation to *Seek justice, encourage the oppressed* (1:16-17).

In this book called "The Gospel of the Old Testament" is sounded one of the most compelling invitations of the Bible: *"Come now, let us reason together," says the Lord. "Though your sins are like scarlet, they shall be as white as snow; though they are red as crimson, they shall be like wool"* (v. 18). This invitation declares the astonishing fact that God, the Creator of the cosmos, cares for us. He loves us and calls us back to Himself even when we have forgotten and forsaken Him. He has bestowed upon each of His children the gift of reason and if we will exercise it we will be led to discover His love and His way for us.

The royalty of Isaiah's day wore robes dyed deep scarlet and crimson. In one of the most beautiful statements of the Bible, God promises His rebellious children of all ages that, though our sin be deep dyed as scarlet or crimson, He will make our hearts as white as snow or wool. The Suffering Servant, later to be identified by the prophet, will be the means of this cleansing. *I will thoroughly purge away your dross and remove your impurities* (v. 25) is the promise of God to the one who repents and returns to Him. *I will . . . remove all your alloy* is the rendering of the *Revised Standard Version.*

When silver was refined and the dross skimmed off the surface, the refiner could then see himself mirrored in the purified metal. When the Divine Refiner removes the dross of sin from our lives, then our purified lives will reflect the very image of God.

This first chapter of Isaiah is as a synopsis of the entire book. It presents the prophet's mission and his message of judgment and redemption. Though he saw "through a glass darkly" that which would later be revealed on Calvary, he proclaims the stupendous message of God as a sorrowing yet loving Father who calls His rebellious children to return to Him.

The message of Isaiah is all too relevant in our day of turbulence, political chaos, and moral breakdown.

GOD OF INFINITE LOVE, SPEAK AGAIN THROUGH YOUR PROPHET OF OLD TO MY HEART AND NEED.

3

GOD'S NEW AGE

READ ISAIAH 2:1–4:2

WE HEAR A GREAT DEAL about "the new age," a sophisticated movement of our time, an eclectic type of religion. It has become one of the hottest topics in books and magazines, and for discussion in Christian circles. This false religion is leading many astray and poses one of the most subtle challenges to Christianity. But the Book of Isaiah proclaims the true new age, God's glorious age of the future.

Isaiah presents God's new age with a sevenfold repetition of *In the last days* or its equivalent (2:11, 17, 20; 3:7, 18; 4:1-2). Universal justice and peace will be its hallmarks.

The hope for a world without war has captured the imagination of peace and political movements throughout the world. The gift of a monument from none other than Russia to the United Nations has the classic text from Isaiah engraved on it: *They will beat their swords into plowshares and their spears into pruning hooks. Nation will not take up sword against nation, nor will they train for war anymore*

(2:4). This noble passage, also quoted by Micah (4:3), articulates man's deep and immemorial longing for peace. True and lasting peace will only come in God's new age.

Man has conquered space, walked on the moon, and developed a fantastic technology. But humankind still has not learned how to live together in peace. War and violence dominate the headlines of our day. Isaiah's sublime vision of the future offers the only and ultimate hope for mankind. God has a new age coming. It will be an age of justice and peace, with a true united nations, people bonded together not by a paper treaty, but by faith and love.

From Revolt to Ruin

In contrast to God's new age, the prophet in these early dark and dismal chapters describes the destruction that will come upon Israel for its sin (2:6–4:1). The pages of history are littered with the wreckage of once-prospering civilizations that came to ruin. Drunk with their own power and vice, they forsook God.

Scathing judgment is pronounced upon the corrupt rulers (3:14-15). God holds leaders accountable for the offices entrusted to them.

Millions of viewers around the world watched on television the swearing in of George Bush as President of the United States. We witnessed his very first act being that of taking a sheet of paper out of his pocket, and in reading it he led his nation in prayer: "Make us strong to do Your work, willing to heed and hear Your will. Write on our hearts these words: Use power to help people. For we are given power not to advance our own purposes, nor to make a great show in the world, nor a name. There is but one use of power, and it is to serve people. Help us remember, Lord."

Washington is known as a pinnacle of political power, a showplace of marble monuments and memorials. Some view it as the Sodom and Gomorrah of politics. But how reassuring it was in that moment to see in that solemn ceremony in our nation's capital an eloquent witness of our motto, "In God We Trust." The true measure of a nation's greatness is not the sum of its possessions, the power of its armaments, or its GNP. The true greatness of a people is reckoned in faith, righteousness, and justice. The leaders of Isaiah's day had forgotten that leadership is a sacred trust.

Womanhood and the Nation

We see in Isaiah (3:16–4:1), as in Amos (4:1-3), a blistering judgment upon the luxury-loving women whose degeneration helped lead the nation to ruin. Their haughtiness and coquettishness was repulsive to God. No less than twenty-one items of vanity are listed in Isaiah 3:18-23. These ornamentations, symbols of their pride, read like a boutique's inventory.

But their pride will bring upon them *instead of fragrance . . . a stench . . . instead of fine clothing, sackcloth; instead of beauty, branding.* The loss of men in war will be a further calamity for these vain and lustful dowagers of Israel.

The quality of its womanhood will always influence greatly the character and destiny of a nation. They are called to be the keepers and guardians of the springs of life. Their tenderness and sensitivity and love are needed to keep the heart of the world from hardening and corruption.

The Branch of the Lord

Isaiah prophesies the coming of the Messiah as the Branch of the Lord (4:2). From the stump of Israel He will come forth with beauty, life, fruitfulness, and glory.

Lord, may I by my life and work help to usher in Your great and glorious new age.

4

Song of the Vineyard

Read Isaiah 4:2–5:30

YOU MAY NEVER have your name in *Who's Who,* but there is a far more important book for you to be recorded in: the *Book of Life.* There will be a remnant, Isaiah prophesies, whose names are recorded. This theme of a Book of Life is found elsewhere in the Bible: Exodus 32:32; Daniel 12:1; Malachi 3:16; Luke 10:20; Revelation 5:8. There will be a day of accountability for our life here on earth. May we be found, in the words of the old hymn, "with our name written there, on the page bright and fair."

God calls us to be a holy people. The hallmark of the faithful ones will be holiness. Holiness is an unalloyed love for God, an unreserved commitment to God and an unbroken fellowship with God. The highest privilege and priority for every Christian believer is holiness of life.

Song of the Vineyard

The prophet's celebrated Parable of the Vineyard is set in the poetic beauty of a song:

> *I will sing for the one I love a song about his vineyard: my loved one had a vineyard on a fertile hillside. He dug it up and cleared it of stones and planted it with the choicest vines. He built a watchtower in it and cut out a winepress as well. Then he looked for a crop of good grapes, but it yielded only bad fruit* (5:1-2).

Great care and provision over a long period was required to build a vineyard. Digging in the rocky soil and irrigating the arid ground of Palestine was hard work. Walls and watchtowers were erected. The extensive labor and care created expectation of a good harvest. But the parable states that the Lord's vineyard "yielded only bad fruit."

The ballad of the vineyard is a love song. It speaks of God's infinite love for humankind. His people were His "vineyard." He had reason to expect good fruit from them. Because they spurned His love and showed ingratitude, God rejected them. They would become as a deserted vineyard, arid and choked with the weeds of their evil doings. The person who shows contempt for the loving-kindness of God will become a spiritual wasteland, fruitless and doomed to destruction.

Contemporary Sins and Consequences

Isaiah pronounces a series of six woes for specific wrongdoings. The first sin and woe deals with greed, with the acquisition of more than is needed at the expense and impoverishment of others (5:8). In our country of affluence we do not need to look far to see the same sin and rapacity of the wealthy as many go hungry and homeless and live in deprivation. God in reproaching this sin warns that a day of accounting will come (v. 9). Let those who are obsessed with real estate and riches take heed.

The second woe of drunkenness (vv. 11-14) has become one of the worst curses in our land. Millions suffer abuse, poverty, and tragedy from alcoholism. Vast sums of money as well as innumerable lives are squandered on alcohol. Not only the addict but other innocent victims among family, friends, and society suffer from this curse. Intoxicated drivers murder over 25,000 persons a year on our highways and maim countless more. It is one of the great scourges in our country and yet we tolerate dishonest advertising lauding the use of alcohol. A man nominated by President George Bush for the United States cabinet post of the Secretary of Defense was rejected by the Senate because of, among other reasons, a reported history of drunken behavior. "Man will be brought low" (v. 15) by alcohol is as true today as it was in the time of Isaiah.

The sins of Isaiah's day as outlined in the final four woe sayings are up-to-date sins of our day. We too live in a world of deceit and skepticism (vv. 18-19), with the lack of moral sense of those "who call evil good and good evil" (v. 20). We also have among us those "who are wise in their own eyes" (v. 21). We too painfully witness the perversion of justice with those "who acquit the guilty for a bribe, but deny justice to the innocent" (v. 23).

Each sin Isaiah names has its counterpart in our society and world today. God's mercy for the repentant is everlasting, but so are His judgments upon sin (vv. 24-30).

FATHER GOD, FOR TIMES LIKE THESE, WE NEED A SAVIOR. HELP US TO BE A FAITHFUL AND FRUITFUL LABORER IN YOUR VINEYARD.

5

Isaiah's Three Looks

Read Isaiah 6

The sixth chapter of Isaiah describes Isaiah's soul-shaking encounter with the glory and holiness of God and the commissioning of this prince of the prophets.

Crisis

In the year that King Uzziah died launches this diary of the prophet's encounter with God. Tradition suggests that Isaiah may have been a nephew of King Uzziah. The king's death was a historical landmark in Israel. It marked the end of a long and prosperous reign of military conquests, agricultural advances, and impressive building, mining, and maritime enterprises (2 Chron. 26:6-15). Though there was the appearance of outward prosperity, there was inward corruption in the soul of the nation. Also, there was now the ominous march of Assyria toward conquest of the whole fertile crescent with Judah in its path.

God comes with a deeper clarity and closeness in the

crises of life. Joni Eareckson Tada testifies: "My paralysis has drawn me close to God and given a spiritual healing which I wouldn't trade for a hundred active years on my feet." Fulton Sheen records in his autobiography: "The greatest gift of all may have been His summons to the cross, where I found His continuing self-disclosure." The turning point in the life of Martin Luther came when his friend, Alexis, struck by lightning, fell dead at his feet.

Sickness, adversity, death, a crossroads – can become spiritual landmarks where we may hear and heed the call of God. C.S. Lewis reminds us that "God whispers to us in our pleasures, but shouts in our pains."

The Upward Look

Isaiah comes to the temple to find guidance for difficult days ahead. Suddenly the resplendent temple is transformed into the very throne room of God. In his moving spiritual autobiography, Isaiah exultantly exclaims, *I saw the Lord seated on a throne, high and exalted.* Seraphim veil their faces as the very foundations of the temple vibrate before His majestic splendor.

The inspired Gospel writer in quoting from Isaiah's prophecy states that this theophany, this appearance of Deity, was none other than Christ Himself who came before the stricken gaze of the prophet: *Isaiah said this because he saw Jesus' glory and spoke about Him* (John 12:41). To the Prophet Isaiah was vouchsafed a vision of the preincarnate Christ, enthroned and exalted in glory.

Holy, holy, holy is the Lord Almighty; the whole earth is full of His glory proclaim these six-winged creatures around the throne of God. Holiness is the essential nature of God.

The Inward Look

Woe to me is the heart cry of Isaiah as he stands before the thrice-holy God. In the light of God's holiness he is overwhelmed with a sense of his own unworthiness.

Isaiah confesses *I am a man of unclean lips and I live among a people of unclean lips.* The discovery of God leads to self-discovery. Our awareness of need must precede God's work in us.

God's response to Isaiah is immediate and remedial. One of the seraphim touches his lips with a glowing ember from the altar, with the altar emblematic of the cross and the live coal of the Holy Spirit. Both pardon and purity are prerequisites for the servant of God. *Your guilt is taken away and your sin atoned for* is the assuring word that comes to Isaiah.

The Outward Look

When cleansed, Isaiah could then hear God's voice calling, *Whom shall I send? And who will go for Us?* The call of God is always wedded to a task. Isaiah responds, *Here am I. Send me!*

God then commissions the prophet, *Go and tell.* What a message it would be. His message of God's redeeming love and the new age to come would resonate through the centuries.

God did not call Isaiah to an easy task. It was to be a prolonged mission to a scoffing generation who would have a fatal immunity to the truth.

The voice of God still calls for proclaimers of His message of love. The hallmark of holiness is a concern for souls outside of Christ. God leads us from salvation to sanctification to service; from pollution to purity to passion.

To follow Christ is still a costly business. He calls us not to success, but to faithfulness; not to security, but to sacrifice; not to comfort, but to a cross.

Holy God, here am I, use me.

6

The Promise of Immanuel

Read Isaiah 7–8

Panic and terror swept both the royal court and the nation as Judah was threatened by Assyrian invasion (7:2). The era of Assyrian expansion marked the last years of Israel as a nation. Dark days of desolation and doom were in store.

"Keep Calm"

Into this darkness God sent Isaiah with a message of hope. The prophet confronts the king as he is inspecting the defenses of his water supply. Isaiah seeks to drive home the truth that true defense is in God.

The prophet's first counsel from God to the king is one of encouragement: *Keep calm and don't be afraid. Do not lose heart* (7:4). To "keep calm" in the midst of crisis can seem next to impossible. But it becomes possible to do just that when we confront the crisis in the confidence and strength of God.

Isaiah counseled the king not to trust in an alliance with

King Tiglath-pileser of Assyria, but to put his trust in God. Ahaz rejects the prophet's message. In response to Ahaz's obstinacy, Isaiah prophesies the invasion and rape of the land and the devastation that would overtake the nation (7:18–8:22).

The Sign of the Virgin Birth

But now, in this hour of crisis, the Lord is about to give an extraordinary sign. "Hear now" proclaims the prophet, calling the nation "to pay attention" to God's promise of great magnitude. The context alerts the reader that this is to be no ordinary announcement. Isaiah flings out his celebrated words: *Therefore the Lord Himself will give you a sign: The virgin will be with child and will give birth to a son, and will call him Immanuel* (7:14). This was God's statement of His extraordinary provision for ultimate deliverance of His people.

The word *almah,* translated "virgin" is believed by many scholars to foreshadow or prophesy the virgin birth of Christ. This is the interpretation by the Gospel of Matthew which quotes this verse on the birth of Christ: *All this took place to fulfill what the Lord had said through the prophet: "The virgin will be with child and will give birth to a son, and they will call Him Immanuel"–which means, "God with us"* (1:22-23). Dr. Luke in his Gospel also attests to the virgin birth of Jesus Christ (1:27).

The doctrine of the Virgin Birth has been a battlefield of theological controversy over the years. Biologically, a virgin birth is an impossibility. But so was the raising of Lazarus and the Resurrection. And what about God's original creation of Adam and Eve without earthly parentage? Can we accept the greater miracle and deny the lesser? In harmony with God's miraculous power, the Virgin Birth would be but one of a chain of supernatural events in the marvelous life of our Lord. Someone has said, "The presence of mystery is the footprint of the Divine."

Immanuel—"God with Us"

In the Gospel account, the angel, in announcing Christ's birth, to Joseph quotes Isaiah that Christ will be called *Immanuel.* Christ alone, in all history, could fill the glowing meaning of this name, *God with us.* Christ was the heart of God wrapped in human flesh. From that feeding trough in the cattle shed of lowly Bethlehem, the cry from that Infant's throat broke through the silence of centuries. For the first time on Planet Earth, there was heard the voice of God from human vocal cords. *Immanuel* speaks to us of the mighty miracle and marvel of God becoming man and dwelling among us.

This thought of God living and walking the earth in human form staggers the imagination. Yet that is precisely what happened at the Incarnation. Christ was God walking the earth in sandals. He alone, of all men, could claim, "Anyone who has seen Me has seen the Father" (John 14:9).

How reassuring to know that this radiant title of Christ first presented by Isaiah is God's promise to us today. Christ is still *Immanuel* to His followers. He is still *God with us.* We have His precious promise, "Surely I will be with you always, to the very end of the age" (Matt. 28:20). We follow the One who said, "Never will I leave you; never will I forsake you" (Heb. 13:5). As God with us, we are superior to all life's vicissitudes, surviving death itself.

And wonder of wonders, you and I can know the reality of Immanuel far more than the Prophet Isaiah could ever have dreamed.

Immanuel, God with us, dwell within me and fulfill the glowing meaning of Your name in my life.

7

WONDERFUL COUNSELOR

READ ISAIAH 9:1-6

NEVERTHLESSS, THERE WILL BE no more gloom is the welcome announcement that opens the ninth chapter of Isaiah. The gloom and doom of the previous chapters give way to a new dawning as Isaiah gives us one of the greatest messianic passages in the Old Testament: *The people walking in darkness have seen a great light; on those living in the land of the shadow of death a light has dawned* (9:2).

In sublime poetic expression the prince of the prophets defines the great light that has come into the world as the Peerless One of history: *For to us a child is born, to us a son is given, and the government will be on His shoulders. And He will be called Wonderful Counselor, Mighty God, Everlasting Father, Prince of Peace. Of the increase of His government and peace there will be no end* (9:6-7).

Each new Advent season, the immortal cadences of this lofty lyric inspire us afresh in the enduring strains of Handel's *Messiah.* Isaiah gives us in this magnificent text a constellation of titles for our Lord. These lofty appellations declare the superlative qualities of the messianic King.

Wonderful Counselor

And He will be called Wonderful Counselor. The traditional *King James Version* separates this designation as two titles, as does Handel in his oratorio which he based on Luther's translation. But more recent Bible scholars regard the comma between them as a translator's error and render it "Wonderful Counselor." This single title also has the support of the ancient Masoretic manuscript as well as the parallel structure of the text.

A counselor is one who advises, provides insight, and guides in directing the judgment and conduct of another. He is involved in the intimacies of life, directing it through its crises and critical periods. Counselors become custodians of the crises of life. Counseling is a staggering and sacred responsibility.

Life is often perplexing, bewildering, complex, problematic, disconcerting. We have an inescapable need for divine guidance. Christ, as Wonderful Counselor, guides us through life's mazes and difficult places.

This Wonderful Counselor is always available, never away, never too busy. He is always as close as the whisper of a prayer. He communes with us through inward promptings, the sensitizing of conscience, the gentle stirrings of His Spirit. And He has left for us His *counselor's manual* for the human heart with the insights and instructions of His inspired Word.

He is compassionate and tender toward us. To Him we are not a case, but a child; not a problem person, but a person with a problem and potential.

Sometimes we find that people entrusted with intimate details of a person's life betray that confidence. But confidentiality is inherent with our divine and Wonderful Counselor.

Some counselors fail because they never achieve a thorough understanding of the person. Motivation and our subconscious dictate much of our conscious life. The inspired chronicler writes: "He knew all men. . . . He knew what was in a man" (John 2:24-25). He fully understands all the subtleties of our emotions, motivation, and subconscious. He is the specialist of the human heart. He is omniscient. He is inerrant in His counsel to us. We may with confidence bring to Him our hurts, failures, deep needs, and aspirations. For Christ is the Wonderful Counselor.

WONDERFUL COUNSELOR, I YIELD MY PERPLEXITY FOR YOUR WISDOM, MY DARKNESS FOR YOUR LIGHT, MY FUTURE FOR YOUR GUIDANCE.

8

The Mighty God

Read Isaiah 9:6-21

And He will be called . . . *mighty God* (9:6). Many have tried to escape the force of this declaration. However, Scripture, history, and human experience corroborate its sacred and sublime truth.

This exalted title speaks of the divinity of Christ. He was the Mighty God in His preincarnate glory and His act of creation. The sacred record declares without equivocation: *Through Him all things were made; without Him nothing was made that has been made* (John 1:3). The same truth is reaffirmed in the Pauline text of Colossians 1:16. He is the Mighty God who tumbled galaxies and solar systems into space, set the stars on their unerring courses, and created the marvelous Planet Earth for us to enjoy.

He is the Mighty God whose birth split time in two. He is the Mighty God in His ministry, miracles, and immortal teachings. He is the Mighty God in His death as our Savior from sin and in His resurrection as He broke the bonds of death. He will be mighty when He comes again in transcendent glory.

Everlasting Father

And He will be called . . . Everlasting Father. A more exact rendering of this verse is Father of Eternity as rendered in the *Amplified Bible.* It presents the staggering truth that Christ is eternal. He had no beginning. He is the great First Cause of all things. He antedates the eons of geological time and the mind-boggling age of the cosmos. He is the timeless One.

Prince of Peace

And He will be called . . . Prince of Peace. Peace may well be the most sought after and at the same time the most elusive treasure. History mocks the effort of world leaders and diplomats on behalf of peace. A famous French historian once computed that there had been 3,130 years of war in contrast to 227 years of peace from the fifteenth century before Christ to his own day. The world had seen 13 years of war for every year of peace. Our own generation has never been without war and turmoil raging somewhere in the world.

Every new generation is born under the ominous cloud that threatens to unleash a nuclear holocaust. We live not only in the age of the split atom but of the split personality as well. Man is beset by neuroses and psychoses that undermine his peace from within. The fears of man are so many and varied that psychologists have charted them all the way from *a* to *z*: from acrophobia, fear of heights, to zoophobia, fear of animals. People cannot sleep, with Americans as the champion insomniacs, consuming billions of pills a year.

The heart of the problem is the problem of the heart. Jesus, the Prince of Peace, enables us to have peace with God by His work of reconciliation. He resolves the inner conflicts and tensions which rob us of peace of mind. He quells the civil war within between the carnal and the spiritual by the work of the Holy Spirit. When we are at peace with God and ourselves then through His grace we will be at peace with others.

These four exalted titles speak to us of four divine attributes of our Lord. *Wonderful Counselor* declares His omniscience, *Mighty God* His omnipotence, *Everlasting Father* His eternity and *Prince of Peace* His omnificence—His unlimited and creative bounty on our behalf.

To Isaiah was given the prophecy of these magnificent titles of our Lord. But to us has been given the Person who fulfilled them. To Isaiah was given the expectation, but to us is given the experience of Christ and the radiant meaning of these titles in our lives.

WONDERFUL COUNSELOR, GUIDE ME; MIGHTY GOD, HOLD ME; EVERLASTING FATHER, KEEP ME; PRINCE OF PEACE, QUIET ME.

9

The Branch That Became the Tree of Life

Read Isaiah 10–11

God's anger has been kindled against Israel for her rejection of His Word and her gross sins. Sin is its own punishment, consuming and destroying, preaches Isaiah, for *Surely wickedness burns like a fire* (9:18). Israel's obstinacy in sin becomes fatal. It is indeed "a fearful thing to fall into the hands of an angry God."

The Fatal Lust for Power

The Assyrian king's arrogance also draws God's wrath and punishment (10:12-19). King Sennacherib's lust for power has its parallels throughout history. We recently observed the fiftieth anniversary of Hitler's barbaric grab for world power that cost 50 million lives in World War II, laid waste the heartland of Western civilization, and spread death and destruction across six of the world's seven continents. Such recent memory makes this passage all too relevant to our day. Dictators and tyrants do not change. Their bombast and violence are the same in every age whether their battles are fought in the eighth century with swords and chariots or in the twentieth century with tanks and missiles. Sennacherib was but one in an unending line of tyrants with a lust for power. We have known all too well those whose "purpose is to destroy, to put an end to many nations" (10:7), who have had their ominous list of cities conquered (v. 9), who "removed the boundaries of nations" and "plundered their treasures" (v. 13).

But in the midst of the prophecy of doom comes Isaiah's recurring reference to the "remnant" who will return (vv. 20-34). God will subdue "in a single day" the enemy of this remnant who "rely on the Lord." The defeat of Israel's oppressors will be no less spectacular than Gideon's victory or the Exodus (v. 26). This prophecy saw remarkable fulfillment when Isaiah records that the angel of the Lord slew in one night with a plague 185,000 troops of the vast Assyrian army (37:36-38; 2 Kings 19:35-37). These accounts reveal that God works in history and the course of events are under His ultimate control.

Promise of the Messiah

Isaiah now leads us from the world powers of man which shall be destroyed to the Lord who will set up the eternal kingdom of God. In this third messianic prophecy of Isaiah, we read: *A shoot will come up from the stump of Jesse; from his roots a Branch will bear fruit* (11:1). The kingly line of David was nothing but a broken, cutoff dynasty. Only a stump was left.

Isaiah prophesies that from this stump of Jesse, David's father, will come a Branch greater than all that grew before it. Springing up from this stump will be a young sapling, bringing renown out of obscurity, life out of death. Centuries later the Apostles Paul and John would quote from this text as messianic prophecies fulfilled by Christ (Rom. 15:12; Rev. 5:5; 22:16).

Christ's birth of the lineage of Jesse was no genealogical accident. History has certain predictable elements under the sovereignty of God. Those who today would publish the obituary of God would do well to ponder the divine thread interwoven through the ages. It has not been severed in this so-called postmodern world. God is still on the throne.

From the stump of Jesse came the Branch that has become the Tree of Life for a lost humanity.

The Peace of the Messiah

God's new age will bring peace between man and nature. Isaiah presents a pastoral picture of an idyllic setting of peace between wild and tame beasts with children.

> *The wolf will live with the lamb, the leopard will lie down with the goat, the calf and the lion and the yearling together; and a little child will lead them* (Isa. 11:6).

The new world, ruled by the Messiah, will be one of justice and righteousness (vv. 3-5). God's new age will be one where *They will neither harm nor destroy on all My holy mountain* (v. 9). This will take place because *the earth will be full of the knowledge of the Lord as the waters cover the sea* (v. 9).

Isaiah's final brush stroke on his masterpiece of the new age adds a dimension of universal peace beyond description, when *the Root of Jesse will stand as a banner for the peoples; the nations will rally to Him, and His place of rest will be glorious* (v. 10).

Miracle of miracles, we can be there. Praise God!

Sovereign God, help me to be an incurable optimist because of what You have in store for us.

10

THE WELLS OF SALVATION

READ ISAIAH 12–30

ISAIAH'S JUBILANT PSALM on the theme of salvation follows naturally the messianic visions of the prophet and word of God's deliverance from the doom of His judgment. His joy becomes irrepressible:

I will praise You, O Lord. . . . Surely God is my salvation; I will trust and not be afraid. The Lord, the Lord, is my strength and my song; He has become my salvation. With joy you will draw water from the wells of salvation. . . . Proclaim that His name is exalted. Sing to the Lord, for He has done glorious things; let this be known to all the world (12:1-5).

Water is essential to life as well as refreshing to our thirst. We could not live for more than a few days without it. How wonderful that something so vital has been provided abundantly by God—in the ground, in our rivers and streams, and by rainfall.

"Water, water, everywhere, nor any drop to drink" were the pathetic lines from Coleridge's *The Rime of the Ancient Mariner*. Man indeed is doomed if he has not water. But there is a water essential to the spiritual life, for its sustenance, survival, and refreshing.

Jesus, in His dialogue with the woman at the well, said, *If you knew the gift of God and who it is that asks you for a drink, you would have asked Him and He would have given you living water* (John 4:10). He added, *Everyone who drinks this water will be thirsty again, but whoever drinks the water I give him will never thirst. Indeed, the water I give him will become in him a spring of water welling up to eternal life* (vv. 13-14).

Jesus gives the water of life to our soul. It springs from the well that was dug deep on a skull-shaped hill. Its healing waters have quenched the deep thirst of humanity that no earthly spring can satisfy. We have with joy drawn water from that well of salvation, provided by the One who is the "Living Water." We too, through Christ, have been delivered from God's judgment on sin. Let us, with the poet prophet of old, rise up with praise and witness to His salvation and glory.

The Days of Judgment

The next section of the Book of Isaiah, chapters 13 to 23, comprises a collection of doom oracles or so-called "foreign prophecies" on nations that were enemies of the people of God. The first is a remarkable prophecy of the desolation of Babylon, "the jewel of kingdoms" (13:19). After painting a scenario of the horrors of its ruin (vv. 6-18), Isaiah prophesies that Babylon "will never be inhabited or lived in through all generations" but will be tenanted only by wild creatures (vv. 20-22). To this day Babylon has remained a heap of ruins and uninhabited since its fall initiated by Cyrus in 539 B.C. Of its haughty kings, the prophet said, *All your pomp has been brought down to the grave* (14:11).

Further edicts of doom follow against Assyria, the Philistines, Moab, Damascus, Cush (Ethiopia), Egypt, Arabia, Tyre, and then unrepentant Judah. *The Interpreters Bible* says of this section of Isaiah, "Any man bold enough to attempt an exposition of these chapters can look for little help from the exegetes, many of whom are frank enough to say, 'We don't know what this means.' " That being also the perception of this writer, we will move through this section expediently to be able to deal in more detail with those highlights of the book that have rich insights and inspiration for us.

CHRIST, THE LIVING WATER, QUENCH THE DEEP THIRSTING OF MY SOUL.

11

THE MISSING KING

READ ISAIAH 20

SARGON, KING OF ASSYRIA, is named in the opening verse of chapter 20. For almost 2,000 years this was the only mention of Sargon's name in ancient literature. Critics said the Bible had blundered; there was no Sargon king of Assyria. Then in 1842 there was the remarkable discovery of the ruins of Sargon's palace in Nineveh, with treasures and inscriptions showing him to have been one of Assyria's greatest kings. Time and again the spade of the archeologist has amazingly supported the accuracy of the Bible.

An anonymous poet reminds us of the enduring quality of God's Word, victorious over all its critics and persecutors through the years:

Last night I passed beside a blacksmith's door,
And heard the anvil ring the vesper chime;
Then looking in, I saw upon the floor
Old hammers, worn with beating years of time.

"How many anvils have you had," said I,
"To wear and batter all these hammers so?"

"Just one," said he, and then, with twinkling eye,
"The anvil wears the hammers out you know."

And so, thought I, the anvil of God's Word,
For ages skeptic blows have beat upon;
Yet though the noise of falling blows was heard,
The anvil is unharmed—the hammers gone.

After two millennia of skepticism and criticism, the archeologist's spade finally turned up the Sargon of Isaiah's inspired manuscript. Like the blacksmith's anvil that wears out all the hammers that have beat against it, so the Bible has outlasted and triumphed over all those who have struck their blows upon it.

A Living Object Lesson

Isaiah is commanded by the Lord to go barefoot and half-naked for three years as a sign and symbol of warning against alliance with Egypt and Ethiopia (chap. 20). Isaiah, gifted of mind and sensitive of soul, was willing to become an object of derision to drive home God's message. He became a walking parable, dressed as a captive to dramatize God's message not to trust the powers of this world which will in the end leave us captive and ashamed.

The Salvation Army in its earlier days often resorted to unconventional means to communicate the Word of God. In those days the Army flourished with souls saved and growth. The unconventional for God became a hallmark of the Army's passion for the lost. Someone has quipped that our Lord uses two figures of speech to describe New Testament evangelism, the figure of the fisherman and of the shepherd—meaning we are to win men "by hook or by crook." There is ever the danger that the church can become keepers of the aquarium instead of fishers of men.

A Sunday School teacher in the nineteenth century took seriously his spiritual responsibility for the young men in his

Bible class. His faithful witness led a Boston shoe clerk to Christ. The teacher's name—Kimball, is virtually unknown. The shoe clerk he led to the Lord became one of the greatest evangelists of all time—Dwight L. Moody. Moody influenced the young preacher Frederick B. Meyer, who converted J. Wilbur Chapman. Chapman arranged for a former baseball player named Billy Sunday to come to Charlotte, North Carolina for revival meetings. The community leaders were so encouraged by the revival that they then brought Mordecai Hamm to town to preach. In his revival a young man came forward and yielded his life to Christ. That young man was Billy Graham who has been used of God to lead millions into the kingdom. It all started with the faithful witness of a simple, obscure man named Kimball.

We never know when we bring our modest offering of loaves and fishes to Christ how much He may multiply them for the blessing of many.

LORD JESUS, HELP ME TO BE A FAITHFUL WITNESS EACH DAY.

12

A Rainbow in the Storm

Read Isaiah 24–30

The End of the World

The next four chapters, are an epilogue to the first twenty-three chapters. It sums up God's judgments on individual nations with a universal punishment for sin: *The earth is defiled by its people. . . . Therefore a curse consumes the earth* (24:5-6). Man's sin corrupts and contaminates not only himself but his environment. *Earth felt the wound* is Milton's poignant statement in his *Paradise Lost,* on the impact on Planet Earth from man's Fall. Man's rebellion against God brings on terrestrial convulsions: *The earth* is broken up and *reels like* a drunkard (v. 20). The ominous threat of nuclear holocaust in our day render's Isaiah's words more than idle speculation.

The Rainbow of Promise

But in the midst of the appalling doom emerge songs of praise to the Lord who is *a refuge for the needy in his distress, a shelter from the storm* (25:4). The Lord is praised who ultimately *will swallow up death forever. The Sovereign Lord will wipe away the tears from all faces* (v. 8). This stupendous promise and daring declaration of the prophet was later echoed in the New Testament and had its fulfillment in our Lord's resurrection and triumph over death.

The darker the storm and clouds, the brighter the rainbow. Here in the midst of the darkest passages of this book shines one of the most radiant gems of the prophet: *You will keep in perfect peace him whose mind is steadfast, because he trusts in You* (26:3). The Hebrew word for "perfect peace" is *shalom,* this rich term repeated twice for well-being, security, and abiding peace.

We are constrained to ask, "Peace, perfect peace, in the midst of the world's tragedies and sorrows?" "Peace, perfect peace, in a world haunted by fear of nuclear holocaust?" "Peace, perfect peace, in a world beset with terrorism, strife, wars, turmoil?"

The words of the song echo our question: "Peace, perfect peace, in this dark world of sin?" Christian experience through the centuries responds that when all is dark and turbulent about us, we can hear the voice of the Master of the storm, saying, "Peace, be still." Peace is not a matter of circumstance, but a matter of the heart. Peace is the Lord's gift to us through His Spirit.

History Is His Story

These passages impart a theology of history. They depict the fragile and temporary nature of tyrants and that history's mills "grind slow but wondrous fine." God is sovereign and the course of events are under His control and will fulfill His ultimate plan for man. There will be a day of accountability and judgment for all nations and people.

History is His story and *All this comes from the Lord Almighty, wonderful in counsel and magnificent in wisdom*

(28:29). Isaiah's message for us is: *In repentance and rest is your salvation, in quietness and trust is your strength* (30:15).

ETERNAL GOD, GRANT TO ME THE STRENGTH THAT COMES IN QUIETNESS AND TRUST, AND THAT PERFECT PEACE THAT COMES FROM A STEADFAST MIND.

13

A Song in the Night

Read Isaiah 30:29

Emerging from Isaiah's lurid scenes of doom is the lyrical line and the precious promise: *You shall have a song as in the night* (30:29, NKJV). Praise God, in the darkest night He gives a song of hope and deliverance.

Such a golden promise of a song in the night is recorded three times in the Word of God. In the Book of Job we read, *God . . . gives songs in the night* (35:10). The psalmist, in reminiscence, said: *I remembered my songs in the night* (77:6). And God promises here through the utterance of Isaiah, *You shall have a song as in the night.*

The Bible and history resonates with this truth that God gives songs in the night seasons. Most of the Psalms of David were composed in times of trouble and trial. Paul and Silas in prison at midnight, sang praises that pierced the very heart of their jailer and constrained him to cry out, "What must I do to be saved?"

Fanny Crosby's hymns have inspired millions. She was

incredibly prolific, composing over 6,000 hymns. She has enriched our singing with such lyrics as "Blessed Assurance," "Jesus, Keep Me Near the Cross," "To God Be the Glory." She did her composing in a dark room. Fanny Crosby was blind. But God lit a light in her mind and soul that enabled her to see and share "rivers of pleasure" and "visions of rapture."

Negro spirituals have been called "pain set to music." Out of the unspeakable suffering of black Americans have come such enduring strains as "Nobody Knows the Trouble I've Seen," and "He Never Said a Mumblin' Word."

Many of the great poets learned in suffering what they taught in song. An anonymous poet has said it this way:

Many a rapturous minstrel
Among the sons of light,
Will say of his sweetest music,
"I learned it in the night."
And many a rolling anthem
That fills the Father's throne,
Sobbed out its first rehearsal
In the shade of a darkened room.

From the pages of Isaiah comes to each of us this radiant promise that God gives songs in the night. Like the refrain from Andrew Lloyd Webber in *The Phantom of the Opera,* God in effect is saying, "I compose the songs in the night." As the hymn reminds us, "There is never a day so dreary, never a night so long,/But the soul that is trusting Jesus will somewhere find a song."

When dark shadows fall across our pathway and we come to a night season, let us take heart and listen, for God has a song for us. He is the God who turns sorrows into symphonies.

GOD, COMPOSER OF THE SONGS IN THE NIGHT, HELP ME TO HEAR AND TAKE HEART FROM THE SONG YOU WILL SEND TO ME IN MY NIGHT SEASONS.

14

STREAMS IN THE DESERT

READ ISAIAH 31–35

ISAIAH KNEW WELL THE FIERCE, blinding sandstorms and the burning heat of the desert. The only shelter and bulwark would be the lee and shadowed side of a rock. There one could find shelter and safety. For the believer, assaulted by life's storms and stresses, our Lord has become *a shelter from the wind and a refuge from the storm . . . the shadow of a great rock in a thirsty land* (32:2). His waters of refreshment and restoration shall never run dry even amid the most barren of life's circumstances.

Mrs. Charles Cowman found in this text the title for her renowned devotional book, *Streams in the Desert.* She shares that she and her beloved husband, as missionaries in the Orient, were serving in the remote mountains of Japan when "one evening, like a bolt out of the blue, came the stroke that completely changed everything in our lives. A doctor was summoned hastily, and after a hurried examination he said to me, 'Your husband's work is finished. Take him to the homeland immediately if you would not bury him in heathen soil.'

"What a change for this keen, active man! From the din of the battle to the seclusion of the sick chamber. From the glow and glory of the work he loved so dearly, to the utter abandonment of it all. A triumphant faith was needed just then and God gave it. My husband found it was possible to praise God in the darkest hour and it was my privilege to be by his side through the six long, pain-filled years.

"One day, when lonely and bereft, a sweet Voice whispered to me, 'Pass on to the troubled hearts some of the messages that were helpful to you throughout the years of testing.' So a book was compiled and the first edition of *Streams in the Desert* was sent on its errand of love."

The rest is literary history. My personal copy of many years is listed as the forty-fifth edition. It echoes Isaiah's timeless truth that God's streams will flow through the deserts of our pilgrimage, quenching the deep thirstings of our lives.

Fanny Crosby was also inspired by this text to compose her lyric sung around the world:

A wonderful Savior is Jesus, my Lord,
A wonderful Savior to me;
He hideth my soul in the cleft of the rock
Where rivers of pleasure I see.

He hideth my soul in the cleft of the rock
That shadows a dry, thirsty land;
He hideth my life in the depths of His love,
And covers me there with His hand.

When we may be called upon to go through the desert experience of life, may we claim God's gracious promise and provision of His refreshing streams in the desert.

HEAVENLY FATHER, THANK YOU FOR THE REFRESHING STREAMS IN THE DESERT PLACES OF OUR LIVES, AND FOR THE REFUGE AMID THE STORMS.

15

GOD'S NEW WORLD ORDER

READ ISAIAH 32–35

CHAPTER 32 OF ISAIAH prophesies the transformation of society. The blessings promised will have their true fulfillment only with the coming of the future King whose reign will bring justice and righteousness, with God's people dwelling in peace and security (32:16-20). It will be a time when all persons and things will be seen in their true light (vv. 3-8). The transformation will result from the outpouring of the Holy Spirit (v. 15).

In the meantime, we are called to live in this world amid its testings and conflict. The Christian pilgrim makes his daily prayer, *Be our strength every morning* (33:2). The ultimate glowing promise for the end of his journey is, *Your eyes will see the King in His beauty and view a land that stretches afar* (v. 17). Our finite imagination cannot begin to grasp the ineffable splendor and majesty of the Christ we shall someday behold and of His vast kingdom that stretches through the unending reaches of time and space.

Chapters 34 and 35 present the two sides of God's judgment: the punishment of the wicked and the promise of the righteous, the woe of the unbeliever and the zeal of the people of God. *The desert shall rejoice and blossom . . . abundantly* (35:1-2, RSV) is the prophet's proclamation. In the transformed world the people of God *will see the glory of the Lord, the splendor of our God* (v. 2). With the promise of ultimate redemption and God's new age, the people are encouraged to: *Strengthen the feeble hands, steady the knees that give way; say to those with fearful hearts, "Be strong, do not fear; your God will come"* (vv. 3-4). Once again the prophet employs his beautiful metaphor of streams in the desert (v. 6), reminding us that God has a new age that will dawn and flourish for those faithful to Him.

THE WAY OF HOLINESS

In one of the choicest texts of the Bible, Isaiah lyricizes the day of the church triumphant.

> *A highway will be there; it will be called the Way of Holiness. The unclean will not journey on it; it will be for those who walk in that Way; wicked fools will not go about on it. . . . But only the redeemed will walk there. . . . Gladness and joy will overtake them, and sorrow and sighing will flee away* (vv. 8-10).

Holiness is not "having arrived." It is not a place but a path on which we continue to journey. It is not a state but a lifetime walk.

In the "New Jerusalem" there will be unblemished purity, and unrestrained joy and gladness. There is indeed a new age coming. It is God's new age. May we as children of God be heirs to its sublime fellowship and felicity.

HOLY GOD, HELP ME TO SO LIVE IN HOLINESS THAT I WILL SOMEDAY BEHOLD THE KING IN HIS BEAUTY AND LIVE IN HIS PRESENCE FOREVER.

16

In God We Trust?

Read Isaiah 36–39

THIS BRILLIANT HISTORICAL narrative with its vivid account conveys the drama and the tension of three memorable events.

In God We Trust?

Sennacherib, king of Assyria, invades Judah and, after capturing a number of cities, encircles Jerusalem with his menacing army. The spokesman for the mighty Assyrian army hurls his challenge in terrifying language while the citizens from the walls listen in stunned silence.

King Hezekiah turns to Isaiah, who assures him that God will intervene and deliver Jerusalem. The king himself then performs the rituals of repentance and prays a noble prayer for God's deliverance from the enemy outside his gates.

God's miraculous intervention results in the destruction of Sennacherib's army in one night by the angel of the Lord. The historian Herodotus says the miraculous destruction was due to a plague brought into the camp by mice. The astounding miracle, by whatever means, is recorded no less than three times, in Isaiah 36–37; 2 Kings 18:13–19:20; 2 Chronicles 32.

The narrative is not without its vital insights and life-lessons. Is there not an echo in the field commander's taunt to Hezekiah when he asks, *On what are you basing this confidence of yours?* The Assyrian then derides any trust in Jehovah by citing Judah's disloyalty: *And if you say to me, "We are depending on the Lord our God"–isn't He the One whose high places and altars Hezekiah removed?"* (Isa. 36:4, 7) In other words, how can you have confidence in a God you have spurned?

What about the motto on our national coins, "In God We Trust"? Is that motto not mocked by our materialism, and our putting aside the altars in the name of separation of church and state? Do we also not sometimes seem terribly inconsistent to the enemies of our faith? This ancient text has a vital message for our nation and society today. "In God We Trust" has to be more than a motto on our coins; it must be a mandate for a consistent faith in our daily lives.

In a pivotal moment of the struggle for this nation's birth, Benjamin Franklin called the founding fathers to prayer. "I have lived, sir, a long time," said the venerable Franklin, "and the longer I live the more convincing proofs I see of this truth, that God governs in the affairs of men. And, if a sparrow cannot fall to the ground without His notice, is it probable that an empire can rise without His aid?"

We are a nation that was born and cradled in dependence on God. Let us help make America truly "One nation under God" and a nation whose principles of justice and righteousness will be a witness to all that "In God We Trust."

GOD OF OUR FATHERS, BLESS OUR COUNTRY WITH AN ENDURING COMMITMENT TO FAITH, RIGHTEOUSNESS, AND JUSTICE.

17

The Things by Which We Live

Read Isaiah 38–39

SET YOUR HOUSE IN ORDER; *for you shall die* is the disconcerting message Isaiah gives to Hezekiah (38:1, RSV) in the second episode of these chapters. Hezekiah again takes his distress to the Lord and pleads to God to spare him from death in return for a vow. Through Isaiah God tells Hezekiah of his reprieve from death and gives him another fifteen years of life.

Life is frail, fragile, and finite. We will not have such a summons as came to Hezekiah, but we will always be but a heartbeat away from death. The invincible reaper knocks ultimately, and often unexpectedly, at every door. We need always to have our "house set in order," for we know not what moment our fragile life may be ushered into eternity.

Following his recovery, Hezekiah composes a psalm. He records, *by such things men live* (v. 16). The king was referring to the promises and gracious acts of God.

We are led to ask ourselves, "What are the things by which I live? Do I live by life's true essentials or have I become caught up with the peripheral rather than the central, the material rather than the spiritual, the trivialities rather than the treasures, the ephemeral rather than the eternal?"

When, as Hezekiah, we come face to face with death and the finality of life, we gain a new perspective on what really matters. The truly successful person is the one who perceives life's true values and meaning and orders life accordingly.

The Treasures in Our House

The final episode in the trilogy of historical incidents recorded in these several chapters is the ambassadors' visit to Hezekiah, bearing gifts from Babylon. After their departure, Isaiah asks, "What have they seen in your house?" The question implies the prophet's disapproval of the king's diplomacy.

Hezekiah's reply confirms Isaiah's fears: *They have seen all that is in my house; there is nothing in my storehouses that I did not show them* (39:4, RSV). Hezekiah, flattered by this attention from Babylon, shows off all his court and treasures. Isaiah then delivers the remarkable prophecy of the Babylonian Captivity, when the king's descendants and everything from Jerusalem's palace would be carried away to Babylon.

"What have they seen in your house?" is a question with great relevance. As others come into our home, what do they see? Do they see merely the material, a pride of possessions? Or do they see the spiritual values that give meaning and foundation to life? Do they see Christ—His spirit and love—in our homes? As with the king of old, our destiny is seen in the intimate setting of our home and family.

May our answer to that probing question reflect a dedication of our total life to the eternal things of God.

Eternal God, help me to know what truly matters most in life, and to order my life accordingly.

18

Someone Is Coming

Read Isaiah 40:1-11

Isaiah 40 marks a turning point in mood and message. The exalted prophetic poetry of this next section lyricizes the grand themes of God's new age, His majestic attributes and works. Isaiah's mighty manuscript here presents the Suffering Servant on the stage of world history.

In our introduction to Isaiah we addressed the theory of a "Deutero-Isaiah," that of a second author for the final twenty-seven chapters. On the basis of historical and biblical evidence we dismissed that theory as a figment of modern criticism. The Book of Isaiah is not a patchwork. In Jesus' day and in our own, it is one book, a unity of prophecy and proclamation.

Someone Is Coming!

Comfort, comfort My people, says your God (40:1) is the opening of this major division of the book that heralds the coming of the Lord. There is to be a preparation:

> *A voice of one calling: "In the desert prepare the way for the Lord; make straight in the wilderness a highway for our God. Every valley shall be raised up, every mountain and hill made low; the rough ground shall become level, and the glory of the Lord will be revealed, and all mankind together will see it. For the mouth of the Lord has spoken"* (vv. 3–5).

This text resonates from Handel's enduring *Messiah* and is quoted in all four Gospels in reference to the ministry of John the Baptist as prophetic of the advent of Christ (Matt. 3:3; Mark 1:3; Luke 3:4-6; John 1:23). Thus it is Christ, the Messiah, of whom Isaiah writes in unforgettable words.

The Transient and the Timeless

All men are like grass, and all their glory is like the flowers of the field (Isa. 40:6) declares the poet-prophet. Indeed, man is but a transient being whose life quickly fades away like the grass, and his glory is short-lived like the flowers of summer.

In contrast, *the word of our God stands forever* (v. 8). Man is transient, God's Word is timeless. Man is ephemeral, God's Word is eternal. Man is fleeting, God's Word is forever. Man is impermanent, God's Word is imperishable. The Bible, with its treasured truths and peerless promises, is God's love letter to humankind.

Thus Isaiah's message comes to us with the divine imprimatur upon every verse and promise. It is the cosmic compass by which we can chart life's direction and destiny.

The Caring Shepherd

A beautiful and tender portrait of God the Creator is depicted in the imagery of the shepherd:

> *He tends His flock like a shepherd: He gathers the lambs in His arms and carries them close to His heart; He gently leads those that have young* (40:11).

In the day of the prophet there could have been no more tender portrait of God than that of the shepherd and his care of the sheep. How assuring and comforting to know that the mighty Creator is to us a shepherd, tenderly caring for us, carrying us "close to His heart."

Several centuries before Isaiah the psalmist had affirmed, "The Lord is my shepherd." And seven centuries after Isaiah there walked the dusty roads of Galilee the One who became the Good Shepherd, who gave His life for His sheep.

When touring the famed St. Calixtus Catacombs in Rome, our attention was captivated by the third-century paintings on the rock walls. They bore a revealing testimony to the life and faith of the early Christian church. Among those rare paintings was one of Christ as the Good Shepherd, carrying a sheep over His shoulder. This concept of Christ as the Good Shepherd has been one of the most endearing portraits of our Lord through the centuries. It eloquently speaks to us of the love, sacrifice, and continued care Christ has for each of us in His flock.

GOOD SHEPHERD, LEAD ME IN THE GREEN PASTURES AND THE STILL WATERS FOR THE NOURISHMENT AND REFRESHMENT OF MY SOUL.

19

The Incomparable God

Read Isaiah 40:12-31

Isaiah proclaims in lofty lyrics the unique and incomparable God of creation, compared to whom the nations and empires of earth are *like a drop in a bucket or as dust on the scales* (40:12-15).

To whom, then, will you compare God? (v. 18) challenges the prophet. He satirizes the manufacturers of idols (vv. 19-20) and eulogizes the glory of God who stretches out the heavens like a canopy. . . . *Lift your eyes and look to the heavens,* summons Isaiah. *Who created all these? He who brings out the starry host one by one, and calls them each by name. . . . not one of them is missing* (vv. 22, 26).

All the revelations of modern science but add to our awe of God as Creator of the fantastic wonders of the universe. Isaiah calls us to an adequate theology and to a recovery of the awesome transcendence of God. "Discover the solemn majesty and ravishing mystery of the Triune God," enjoins A.W. Tozer. He adds, "We may live a full lifetime and die without once having our minds challenged by the sweet mystery of the Godhead, at contemplation and utterance of His majesty." If we can be assured of God's sovereignty over the universe, then surely we can trust Him with our finite lives.

This magnificent chapter culminates with one of the most sublime and inspiring passages of the Bible:

> *Do you not know? Have you not heard? The Lord is the everlasting God, the Creator of the ends of the earth. He will not grow tired or weary, and His understanding no one can fathom. He gives strength to the weary and increases the power of the weak. Even youths grow tired and weary, and young men stumble and fall; but those who hope in the Lord will renew their strength. They will soar on wings like eagles; they will run and not grow weary, they will walk and not be faint* (vv. 28-31).

God's penman compares the believer who trusts in God to an eagle that soars with unwearying grace and strength. The eagle's noble inheritance is the heights of the heavens. It pierces the eye of the midday sun. It builds its nest in lofty crags where man has not set his foot. It plays with the winds and currents of the air. This majestic specimen is king of the birds.

The eagle soars to great heights, not by the power of his wings, but by surrendering himself to the currents and power of the wind. So it is with the believer. We soar and reach the heights of the spiritual life not by our own finite power, but by surrendering to the mighty power of the Holy Spirit.

Joni Eareckson Tada has a beautiful recording with the title song, "Spirit Wings." The refrain goes:

> *Spirit wings, you lift me*
> *Over all the earthbound things.*
> *And like a bird my heart is flying free.*
> *I'm soaring on the song of Spirit Wings.*
> *O Lord of all, You let me see*
> *A vision of Your majesty.*
> *You lift me up, You carry me,*
> *On Your Spirit Wings.*

Joni's radiant testimony in song can be the reality for each of us. God has destined us to soar on Spirit Wings. Let us rise up and claim our noble inheritance.

INCOMPARABLE GOD, HELP ME TO SOAR ABOVE EARTHBOUND THINGS TO THE HEIGHTS OF HOLY LIVING AND VISIONS OF YOUR MAJESTY.

20

THE LORD OF HISTORY

READ ISAIAH 41–49

A NEW PERSONAGE EMERGES on the landscape of history, one whom God will stir *up from the east* (41:2). It is a name soon to be whispered in the courts of world powers. In one of the most remarkable prophecies of the Bible, 160 years in advance, Isaiah tells of Cyrus the Great, king of Persia (538–529 B.C.), who would be used as a servant of the Lord to carry out His purposes.

Cyrus became the conqueror of Babylon and ended the captivity of the Jews with a decree that allowed them to return to Jerusalem and rebuild their temple (Ezra 1:1-4; 6:3-5; 2 Chron. 36:22-23). Cyrus is actually named in Isaiah 44:28 and 45:1, as well as referred to in 46:11.

God confirms that He Himself directs the ultimate course of history, exclaiming in reference to the victories of Cyrus: *Who has done this and carried it through? . . . I, the Lord* (41:4). The God of the galaxies is also the God of Planet Earth and His children that He has placed upon it. He is the

Lord of history who uses both His covenant people and a pagan monarch to unwittingly carry out His designs.

My servant (vv. 8-9) is a key term, found twenty times in these next fourteen chapters. It refers here and elsewhere to Israel, at other times to individuals. In the royal terminology of Isaiah's day, "servant" referred to a trusted envoy. We are all called to be servants, to be His trusted envoys to the world around us.

God is the *Redeemer* (v. 14), a title for God that Isaiah records thirteen times. The term was rich in meaning, referring to the nearest kinsman who had the responsibility to rescue a relative or recover a lost inheritance. Further on in Isaiah's writing, God assures His people of His presence amid life's most trying ordeals:

> *Fear not, for I have redeemed you; I have called you by name; you are Mine. When you pass through the waters, I will be with you; and when you pass through the rivers, they will not sweep over you. When you walk through the fire, you will not be burned* (43:1-2).

The ultimate reference to "servant" in Isaiah is to Christ as the Suffering Servant. We encounter the first of the four "servant songs" that refer to Christ in 42:1-9. The others are found in 49:1-13; 50:4-9; 52:13–53:12. The first four verses of chapter 42 are quoted in part by Matthew (12:18-21) as being fulfilled in Christ. This prophecy was also echoed at the baptism of Christ, thus identifying Him with the Suffering Servant of Isaiah.

He is the promised One of whom God says *I will put My Spirit on Him and He will bring justice to the nations* (Isa. 42:1). *A bruised reed He will not break*—from the discordant life He will bring forth harmony. *A smoldering wick He will not snuff out*—He will light up the life whose lamp has almost gone out. He will also be: *a light for the Gentiles, to open eyes that are blind, to free captives from prison and to release from the dungeon those who sit in darkness* (42:3-7).

The Residue for God

In one of Isaiah's many uses of striking imagery he describes a man who takes a log, half of which he burns for fuel and then cooks his meal over it. Then with what was left over *he makes a god, his idol* (44:14-17). The "residue" (KJV) was devoted to his god. It becomes a parable of countless lives for whom utility and comfort take priority.

Isaiah's parable is as up-to-date as tomorrow's newscast. In many lives, God still gets the residue, the leftovers, after personal priorities are met. Charles Wesley gave a positive twist to this concept in his hymn:

Lord, in the strength of grace,
With a glad heart and free,
Myself, my residue of days,
I consecrate to thee.

Jim Elliot reminds us of a timeless truth when he said: "He is no fool who gives what he cannot keep to gain what he cannot lose." When we give God our best and our all, we receive in return the highest dividends of joy, peace, and life abundant and eternal.

Sovereign God, I thank You that You are not a God Emeritus, that You have not taken Your hand off the rudder of the universe, but You are in charge, directing its course and destiny.

21

THE JOY OF AGING

READ ISAIAH 46

"THE GRAYING OF AMERICA" is the phenomenon of the increasingly large segment of the 60+ citizens of our country's population. Gerontologists—those who study aging—point out the stresses and challenges that can accompany the aging process. Concerns deal with health and debilitating diseases, memory loss, the impact of retirement, widowhood and bereavement, residence change and living arrangements. On the plus side, their research indicates that today "old age" starts closer to eighty-five than sixty-five, and these years can be creative and fulfilling.

God through His penman tells us that the decades after sixty need not be a time of stress but rather of strength. *Even to your old age and gray hairs I am He, I am He who will sustain you* (46:4) is God's promise to seasoned citizens. Isaiah's text finds an echo in Robert Browning's lines:

Grow old along with me,
The best is yet to be;

The last of life for which the first was made;
Our times are in His hand
Who saith, "A whole I planned,
Youth shows but half; trust God,
See all, nor be afraid!"

E. Stanley Jones in his book, *Christian Maturity,* shares how this promise of God from Isaiah was fulfilled in his advanced years. He writes that God said to him when he passed seventy: "I'm giving you the best ten years of your life—the next ten ahead." Jones adds: "Two of them have passed and they have literally been the best two years of my life. Eight to go! . . . Practically all my question marks have now been straightened out into dancing exclamation points."

Fellow seasoned citizens, none of us is getting out of this life alive. But let us not settle for an attic full of rusty relics of the past. We can face today and tomorrow with courage and confidence, affirming with the prophet of old that God will sustain us throughout our years.

B.C. Forbes, founder and publisher of *Forbes* magazine, cautioned his readers: "Don't forget until too late that the business of life is not business, but living." Let us give priority to the business of living—living with faith in the God who also has promised, *They will still bear fruit in old age, they will stay fresh and green* (Ps. 92:14). Then we shall truly know the joy of aging!

Eternal God, abide with me when it is toward evening and the day is far spent. Enable us to fight the good fight, to finish the course and to keep the faith to the end.

22

ENGRAVED ON THE PALMS OF HIS HANDS

READ ISAIAH 49:16

GOD'S LOVE AND CARE for His children is expressed in a question by the Lord on the most tender of human relationships: *Can a mother forget the baby at her breast and have no compassion on the child she has borne?*

We know all too well the sad answer to that question. Children throughout the world have been found abandoned or abused by a mother. The Lord Himself responds to the question with a stunning affirmation of His love for us:

> *Though she may forget, I will not forget you! See, I have engraved you on the palms of My hands* (49:15-16).

This is one of the most beautiful portraits of God's love found in the Bible. The most eloquent expressions of His love for us are the nail prints in the hands of our Lord. Christ speaks to us from the ancient text of the poet-prophet and insists He will never forget us, for we are engraved on the palms of His hands. Calvary has established an eternal memorial with God for every believer.

In this poignant passage with its astonishing portrayal of our Lord, we see God's eternal love for us. Those hands pierced for us on Calvary bear the marks of His love and salvation. Those wounds, made for our transgressions, become in the powerful metaphor of the prophet an engraving of our names on the palms of the hands of the crucified Savior.

The simple chorus penned by Albert Orsborn reminds us of this sacred truth:

He cannot forget me, though trials beset me;
Forever His promise shall stand.
He cannot forget me, though trials beset me;
My name's on the palm of His hand.

The story is told of a Russian citizen during the years of the Nazi occupation who had watched his young wife brutalized and killed after her newborn child had been snatched from her arms and given to a youthful officer whose wife was known to be barren. The prisoner gazed for what he thought might be the last time at the wide, bewildered eyes of his only child. Fearful of the days ahead and what cruelties might take from him his fragile mental powers, the prisoner did a startling thing. With his own knife he carved the name of the child in his right hand. Never would he allow himself to forget the object of his love.

The astonishing portrayal by Isaiah reveals a love beyond our powers of understanding or description. But it woos and wins our hearts for time and eternity.

The Suffering Servant

Isaiah, the preeminent poet of the prophets, presents an unrivaled portrait of Christ as the Suffering Servant in these final chapters of his magnificent book. The first of his four "Servant Songs" (42:1-9) celebrated our Lord's character and worldwide mission and is cited by Matthew as fulfilled in the ministry of Christ. The second song of the Servant speaks of His prophetic task to bring light and salvation to the nations (49:1-13).

In this third of the "Servant Songs" (50:4-9), we have our Lord's meditation in the form of a soliloquy on His sufferings. His utterance speaks of the depth of suffering that He endured on His path to the cross: *I offered My back to those who beat Me, My cheeks to those who pulled out My beard; I did not hide My face from mocking and spitting.* This prophecy was fulfilled in tragic detail in the agony and ignominy of Christ's suffering.

In the words of the hymn writer, "Dear Savior, I can never repay the debt of love I owe! Here, Lord, I give myself away; 'tis all that I can do."

23

Steadfast on the Path of the Cross

Read Isaiah 50–52

THEREFORE *HAVE I SET MY FACE like a flint* (50:7) is the prophetic utterance of the Servant. It speaks of the resolution of the Messiah in His mission of suffering and sacrifice. Luke caught this resolution on the part of the Master in recording, just after Christ's prediction of His impending death, *Now it came to pass, when the time had come for Him to be received up, that He steadfastly set His face to go to Jerusalem* (Luke 9:51, JB). Our Lord "set His face like flint" toward the cross that awaited Him at Jerusalem.

Throughout Christian history there have been individuals who remained unswerving in their determination to follow Christ on the pathway of the cross. Martin Luther, his very life in the balance as he stood before his enemies who wanted him out of the way, declared, "Here I stand, I can do no other."

William Booth set his face steadfastly to the task to which God called him. His undaunted battle cry in the face of man's moral and social destitution was, "I'll fight! I'll fight to the very end!"

Dietrich Bonhoeffer reminds us in his classic work, *The Cost of Discipleship,* that "cheap grace is grace without discipleship, grace without the cross." He discourses on costly grace that "costs a man his life." When faced with the savage violence of Hitler's Third Reich, Bonhoeffer wrote from his prison cell: "Who stands fast? Only the man who is ready to sacrifice all when he is called to obedient and responsible action in faith and in exclusive allegiance to God—the responsible man who tries to make his whole life an answer to the question and call of God" (From *Letters and Papers from Prison*).

Bonhoeffer's brilliant theology was not formulated in a vacuum, but was both hammered out and lived under Nazi persecution. In resisting Hitler's atheistic inhumanity, Bonhoeffer himself paid the high cost of discipleship. For his flintlike faith, he was executed by the Nazis when he was only thirty-nine.

There are no bargain rates for Christian discipleship. Christ still calls for steadfast soldiers of the cross. The One who "set His face like a flint" toward His execution on Calvary calls us from the expedience and vacillations of our world to a resolute stand in the faith.

Isaac Watts challenges all of us in his hymn:

Am I a soldier of the cross
A follower of the Lamb,
And shall I fear to own His cause,
Or blush to speak His name?

Must I be carried to the skies
On flowery beds of ease,
While others fight to win the prize,
And sail through stormy seas?

Are there no foes for me to face?
Must I not stem the flood?

Is this vile world a friend to grace,
To help me on to God?

Since I must fight if I would reign,
Increase my courage, Lord!
I'll bear the toil, endure the pain,
Supported by Thy word.

ALMIGHTY GOD, KEEP ME STEADFAST ON THE PATHWAY OF THE CROSS.

24

The Rock from Which We Were Hewn

Read Isaiah 51:1–52:12

ALVIN TOFFLER'S *Future Shock* has enjoyed wide readership since its best-selling advent in 1970. Exploring the impacts of change, it claimed to help readers prepare for their "collision course with the future." It took a different approach than previous social thinkers who drew upon the past to illuminate the present. Toffler in his "Introduction" said, "This book is designed to increase the future-consciousness of its reader. The degree to which the reader, after finishing the book, finds himself thinking about, speculating about, or trying to anticipate future events, will provide one measure of its effectiveness." Ours is an age obsessed with foretellers and forthtellers of the future.

In contrast Isaiah calls his hearers and readers to retrospection, to look to their past in order to understand their present. *Look . . . to the quarry from which you were hewn; look to Abraham, your father, and to Sarah, who gave you birth* (51:1-2). It is a salutary exercise for the soul to recall its spiritual heritage. *The Jerusalem Bible* renders the prophet's challenge: *Look to the rock from which you were hewn* (v. 1).

None of us comes to our faith in a vacuum. We often come to God from the rich heritage of family and church, associations through which God called us and made us heirs of His promises and citizens of the commonwealth of God (v. 8). We each have our spiritual fathers and mothers whom we should remember with gratitude and with motivation to be true to the spiritual legacy they have bestowed.

The *Authorized Version* in verse 2b can lead us also to remember the depths of sin from which God rescued us: *Look . . . to the hole of the pit from which you were dug* (JB). When we remember what God saved us from—our sin and selfishness and lost condition—indeed our hearts must overflow with gratitude for God's grace and goodness.

THOSE WHO BRING GOOD TIDINGS

The Apostle Paul was very familiar with the writings of Isaiah and quotes copiously in his epistle to the Romans, no less than nineteen verses from the prophet. In Romans 10:15 he quotes Isaiah's lofty and lyrical lines:

> *How beautiful on the mountains are the feet of those who bring good news, who proclaim peace, who bring good tidings, who proclaim salvation, who say to Zion, "Your God reigns!"* (Isa. 52:7)

Our world today is bombarded with bad news. The media constantly impinges on us with the violence, the horrors, and the negative events of our world. May we be among those who proclaim peace and the good tidings of salvation. May we be among those who will tell our troubled and tortured world that God still reigns and wants to give us His priceless gift of peace through the atoning sacrifice of His Son Jesus Christ.

ALMIGHTY GOD, KEEP ME FAITHFUL ON THE PATHWAY OF THE CROSS, THAT I MAY RUN WITH PERSEVERANCE THE RACE SET BEFORE ME.

25

THE SUFFERING AND GLORY OF CHRIST

READ ISAIAH 52:13–53:12

THE FIFTY-THIRD CHAPTER of Isaiah ushers us into the holy of holies in the sanctuary of Christ's life. It is the pinnacle of the prophet's writing on the suffering and exaltation of Christ. This best-known and beloved chapter presents in immortal words the sublime sacrifice of Christ for our salvation.

An introduction to chapter 53 is given in 52:13-15 in this fourth of the Servant Songs. The fluid concept of the Servant, which sometimes had referred to Israel, now engenders the prophecy that could only be fulfilled by Christ. The prophet summarizes the exaltation and humiliation of the Servant:

> *See, My servant will act wisely; He will be raised and lifted up and highly exalted. Just as there were many who were appalled at Him— His appearance was so disfigured beyond that of any man and His form marred beyond human likeness.*

This text challenges our often adorned concepts of Calvary. Our gilded and decorated crosses are light years away from this depiction of the One who was *marred* and *disfigured* by the brutality of Calvary. The sleepless night through the trials, the scourging that lacerated His flesh, the crown of thorns that punctured His brow, the mockery and spittle of the mob, the heavy cross on the Road of Sorrows, the nails that tore through His hands and feet, the unquenchable thirst, the spear that pierced His side, the betrayal and desertion of His closest followers, were such that those who looked upon Him in His suffering were *appalled.* But this text also proclaims that *He will be raised up and highly exalted.*

Who has believed our message and to whom has the arm of the Lord been revealed? The opening of the fifty-third chapter indicates many will disbelieve and reject the Messiah.

A Voluntary Offering

Isaiah prophesies of Him: *He grew up before Him like a tender shoot, and like a root out of dry ground* (v. 2). The kingly house of David had been cut down but the Messiah will be the Branch (4:2) and the shoot from the stump of Jesse (11:1).

He had no beauty or majesty to attract us to Him, nothing in His appearance that we should desire Him (53:2). He did not come with royal trappings or supernatural beauty, but in humility and obscurity. Christ the Mighty God laid aside His glory and "emptied Himself" of His incomputable splendor in the miracle of the Incarnation.

He was despised and rejected by men, a man of sorrows, and familiar with suffering. Like one from whom men hide their faces He was despised, and we esteemed Him not (53:3). The Lord of glory came to our planet, not to rule, but to suffer, not to bask in splendor, but to die.

Here the prophet gives us one of the cardinal titles of Christ—*Man of Sorrows.* This title and text speak volumes on His suffering and sacrifice for the world. Some notable men are men of wealth, some are men of fame, some are men of pleasure, but Christ was a Man of Sorrows. He was the Lord of anguish, the King of suffering.

The sorrows of Christ defy description or definition. His love was wounded by betrayal and desertion. His soul suffered the imputed condemnation for man's transgressions. His body felt the torture of the cross. He endured the ignominy, mockery, dereliction, and brutality of Calvary. To what fathomless depths God descended to rescue a dying world!

A Vicarious Offering

In matchless language the prophet proclaims the doctrine of the vicarious sacrifice of the Servant: *He took up our infirmities and carried our sorrows. . . . He was pierced for our transgressions, He was crushed for our iniquities; the punishment that brought us peace was upon Him, and by His wounds we are healed* (53:4-5). *For the transgression of my people He was stricken* (v. 8).

"He was wounded for our transgressions" (NKJV). The nails that tore through His sacred hands and feet were our sins. The thorns that pierced His brow and marred His visage were our sins. The scourge that lacerated the flesh of His back to ribbons was our sins. The wagging heads that mocked Him and the tongues that vilified Him were our sins. He carried our sorrow. He suffered our condemnation. On Calvary's cross He died our death. And *by His wounds we are healed.*

The mournful music on our Lord's vicarious sacrifice deserves to proceed without interruption: *We all, like sheep, have gone astray, each of us has turned to his own way; and the Lord has laid on Him the iniquity of us all* (v. 6).

We are all incalculable debtors to the infinite and sacrificial love of God on our behalf.

Loving God, thank You that Calvary included me—my sin, my guilt, my salvation.

26

A Victorious Offering

Read Isaiah 53:7–55:13

As we pondered Isaiah's matchless passage on the sacrifice of the Son of God, we considered in our last study *A Voluntary Offering* and *A Vicarious Offering*. The poet-prophet culminates his immortal text by proclaiming that the sacrifice of God's Servant is *A Victorious Offering*.

Isaiah writes as though standing at the foot of the cross as he unveils this poignant portrait of the suffering Son of God. The vivid details of his prophecy were all remarkably fulfilled in the passion of our Lord.

A Sublime Silence

Jesus manifested the inward strength of silence both in the interrogation of His trials and on Calvary. The seven sayings from the cross take less than one minute to utter in the original language spoken. Thus, for five hours and fifty-nine minutes of those six hours on the cross, our Lord was silent. Only the very strong and innocent could have the vast self-control to be silent before His accusers under unjust treatment and brutal execution.

Seven centuries earlier, Isaiah prophesied this sublime silence of Christ in His suffering and death: *He was oppressed and afflicted, yet He did not open His mouth; He was led like a lamb to the slaughter, and as a sheep before her shearers is silent, so He did not open His mouth* (53:7).

Even the type of death and burial of the Lord is predicted by this preeminent prophet. *He was assigned a grave with the wicked,* speaks of His crucifixion as a criminal between two other condemned criminals. The Gospels record that Jesus was buried in the tomb of the wealthy Joseph of Arimathea, thus fulfilling Isaiah's striking prophecy: *He was assigned a grave . . . with the rich in His death* (v. 9).

A Victorious Offering

The ultimate word from Isaiah is not of Christ the victim, but of Christ the Victor. The extraordinary vision vouchsafed to the prophet is one of triumph emerging out of tragedy, exaltation out of humiliation, forgiveness out of suffering and death.

The prophet declares that God *will see His offspring and prolong His days, and the will of the Lord will prosper in His hand. After the suffering of His soul, He will see the light of life and be satisfied; by His knowledge My righteous servant will justify many, and He will bear their iniquities. Therefore I will give Him a portion among the great, and He will divide the spoils with the strong, because He poured out His life unto death, and was numbered with the transgressors. For He bore the sin of many, and made intercession for the transgressors* (vv. 10-12).

In the light of the New Testament we know that Good Friday gave way to Easter Sunday, and our Lord's death on Calvary was climaxed by His mighty resurrection and ascension. Christians today celebrate not a crucifixion but a coronation. Christ has been given a name above every name and reigns today in the believer's heart.

In this matchless chapter, Isaiah has led us to Calvary, to stand before one of the most supreme and sacred truths of eternity. It is too deep for us to plumb its mystery and majesty, but with Isaac Watts we are constrained to say:

When I survey the wondrous cross
On which the Prince of Glory died,
My richest gain I count but loss,
And pour contempt on all my pride.

Forbid it Lord, that I should boast
Save in the death of Christ, my God;
All the vain things that charm me most,
I sacrifice them to His blood.

Were the whole realm of nature mine,
That were a present far too small;
Love so amazing, so divine,
Demands my soul, my life, my all.

GOD OF INFINITE LOVE, WHEN I PONDER CALVARY, WITH THE POET I AM CONSTRAINED TO SAY, "LOVE SO AMAZING, SO DIVINE, DEMANDS MY LIFE, MY SOUL, MY ALL."

27

God's Gracious Invitation

Read Isaiah 55:1-11

It is not surprising to find one of the most gracious invitations in the Bible shortly following Isaiah's peerless passage on the vicarious sacrifice of God's Servant.

Come, all you who are thirsty, come to the waters; and you who have no money, come, buy and eat! (55:1)

God's grace and gift of salvation is free to anyone. It satisfies the deepest thirstings of our souls that no earthly spring can slake. It nourishes the deepest hunger of our heart that no earthly bread can satisfy. It refreshes the life as no earthly pleasures can do.

Conditions of God's Grace

But such a priceless gift is conditional. The urgent call of the prophet reminds us that the day of grace will not last forever: *Seek the Lord while He may be found; call on Him while He is near* (v. 6). Some people plan to be saved at the eleventh hour, but die at the tenth! Also, continued rejection of the Lord hardens the heart so that the soul may no longer be sensitive to God's call and grace.

We must not only seek God but must also repent of our sins to know God's gift of salvation and life eternal: *Let the wicked forsake his way and the evil man his thoughts. Let him turn to the Lord, and He will have mercy on him, and to our God, for He will freely pardon* (v. 7).

The eternal God, whose ways and thoughts transcend our finite minds (vv. 8-9), has provided for our pardon and made us heirs of the eternal promises. He has recorded the wonder and wooing of His love in His sacred Word.

We have pondered a text that transcends human language and deserves the eloquence of angels. But we claim the promise given by God's prophet: *My word that goes out . . . will not return to Me empty, but will accomplish what I desire and achieve the purpose for which I sent it* (v. 11).

An unknown poet has penned the truth of salvation by the Savior as proclaimed by the prophet:

I know a soul that is steeped in sin,
That no man's art can cure;
But I know a Name, a Name, a Name,
That can make that soul all pure.

I know a life that is lost to God,
Bound down by things of earth;
But I know a Name, a Name, a Name,
That can bring that soul new birth.

DEAR SAVIOR, HELP ME TO FAITHFULLY SHARE WITH OTHERS YOUR GRACIOUS AND GLORIOUS INVITATION.

28

THE CROWN JEWEL OF THEOLOGY

READ ISAIAH 56–59

A HOUSE OF PRAYER

THERE IS A RELEVANCE for us in the prophet's admonition from God, *For My house will be called a house of prayer for all nations* (56:7). This verse echoes in the New Testament where our Lord utters it in the temple at Jerusalem in His zeal for the sanctity of God's house (Matt. 21:13; Mark 11:17; Luke 19:46).

What of our places of worship? Are they first and foremost "houses of prayer"? Are they places where we meet with God, where we worship and praise Him?

We need such sacred places, set aside for communion with God. The prophet's exhortation and its New Testament setting of the Lord's cleansing of the temple warns us not to let our holy places lose their purpose of divine communion.

THE CROWN JEWEL OF THEOLOGY

God through His spokesman gives us a magnificent self-disclosure: *For this is what the high and lofty One says—He who lives forever, whose name is holy: "I live in a high and holy place, but also with him who is contrite and lowly in spirit, to revive the spirit of the lowly and to revive the heart of the contrite"* (Isa. 57:15). This lofty text of the Bible presents an eloquent anthology of some of the great attributes of God. Compressed in these few lyrical lines is the eternity, holiness, transcendence, and immanence of God.

The text coruscates with the crown jewel of theology—the sublime truth that the God "who inhabits eternity" (RSV) is also the God who "dwells with him who is of a contrite and humble spirit" (RSV). Think of it—the God who created the incomputable reaches of the cosmos condescends to live in my frail and finite life. This incarnational theology of Isaiah has become real through God the Holy Spirit.

The prince of the prophets in this text flings out one of the most stupendous truths known to man—the God of the cosmos in His infinite love condescends to dwell in the life of His followers. Could there ever be a more spine-tingling declaration than that!

Sin, the Great Separator

Isaiah reminds his hearers that their separation from God is caused not by God's impotence but by their sin: *Surely the arm of the Lord is not too short to save, nor His ear too dull to hear. But your iniquities have separated you from your God; your sins have hidden His face from you, so that He will not hear* (59:1-2). It is forever true that if God's presence and prayer are not real to us, sin is the cause. Separation from God and His priceless gift of salvation is the greatest consequence of sin. For to live life without God is to miss life itself.

Lord, who became incarnate in the miracle of Bethlehem, come and be born in the lowly manger of my heart.

29

The Grand Finale

Read Isaiah 60–66

The Culminating Prophecy

Isaiah's magnificent prophecies climax with the glory of the divine presence bursting forth as the radiant dawn for restored Zion and all the peoples of the world. God summons the nations from the moral nihilism and darkness of the previous chapter: *Arise, shine, for your light has come, and the glory of the Lord rises upon you* (60:1). The text is animated with this prophecy of the consummation of history: *Then you will look and be radiant, your heart will throb and swell with joy* (v. 5).

The city, symbolic of the New Jerusalem, spiritual Israel, is depicted with God turning its brass to gold, its iron to silver, its wood to bronze, and its stones to iron. A vast volume of commerce supplies its wants. Its walls will be called "Salvation" and its gates "Praise." But the city's majesty and splendor will be its moral order of peace and righteousness and the divine presence, for *the Lord will be your everlasting light, and your God will be your glory* (v. 19).

Isaiah's sixty-first chapter announces the mission of the One to proclaim the evangel, the bringer of good tidings. This prophecy was hallowed by our Lord when, in His "key-note address" in the synagogue of Nazareth (Luke 4:18-19) He quoted: *The Spirit of the Sovereign Lord is on Me, because the Lord has anointed Me to preach good news to the poor. He has sent Me to bind up the brokenhearted, to proclaim freedom for the captives and release for the prisoners . . . to comfort all who mourn* (Isa. 61:1-2). After reading this text Christ added His arresting claim, "This day is this Scripture fulfilled in your ears."

The Lonely Treader of the Winepress

In a dramatic dialogue the prophet asks, *Who is this coming . . . with His garments stained crimson? Who is this, robed in splendor, striding forward in the greatness of His strength?* The answer ricochets among the heavens, *It is I, speaking in righteousness, mighty to save.*

The prophet is then led to ask, *Why are Your garments red, like those of one treading the winepress?* The answer encompasses all the passion of our Lord in His redeeming work: *I have trodden the winepress,* adding the significant word, *alone* (63:1-3). The winepress, in which the grapes were trodden underfoot to make the wine, left the worker splattered with the juice of crushed grapes. The image became symbolic of the carnage of battle. This metaphorical text has come to represent Christ, the bloodstained but triumphant warrior, returning from battle. As the famous hymn declares, "He hath trampled out the vintage where the grapes of wrath are stored."

John further relates this prophecy and analogy to the passion of our Lord in the final triumph when He appears "dressed in a robe dipped in blood. . . . He treads the winepress of the fury of the wrath of God Almighty" (Rev. 19:13, 15).

When this writer was privileged to interview the late Salvation Army poet, General Albert Orsborn, I asked him about a line of his best known song, *My Life Must Be Christ's Broken Bread.* It is the line, "Beyond the brook His winepress stands." The General responded that it was borrowed from the imagery of this biblical text. The second verse of that "sacramental song of The Salvation Army" calls us to tread with our Lord the winepress of sacrifice:

My all is in the Master's hands
For Him to bless and break;
Beyond the brook His winepress stands
And thence my way I take,
Resolved the whole of love's demands
To give, for His dear sake.

The Grand Finale

Isaiah's final scenario ushers in the dawning of God's new age as the Creator declares, *Behold, I will create new heavens and a new earth* (Isa. 65:17). This declaration is so significant as to be repeated twice in the New Testament (2 Peter 3:13; Rev. 21:1). Idyllic prosperity and peace will reign (Isa. 65:17-25). These final chapters of Isaiah correspond to the closing chapters of the New Testament (Rev. 21–22) in the anticipation of the New Jerusalem, the New Heaven, and the New Earth and the victorious return and reign of Christ.

Any commentator on these texts cannot help but feel he is offering a "teaspoon worth of comment" upon passages that deal with the ocean of infinity. God's new age, and a New Heaven and a New Earth for the redeemed! A fitting climax indeed from this peerless penman of the prophets!

Eternal God, we rejoice for the new age You have promised and pray that by Your grace we may be ready and worthy.

The New Covenant

30

Standing in the Gap

Read Jeremiah 1

JEREMIAH IS THE LONGEST BOOK in the Bible, containing more words than any other, representing almost one twentieth of the entire Bible. In keeping with the turbulence of his time, the book is noted for its lack of a chronological or topical order.

Perhaps no prophet in the Old Testament has been so widely misunderstood. He is known as the "weeping prophet," the prophet of gloom and doom. From him we derive our word "jeremiad," which means a tale of woe.

A Dominant Figure

Our culture of instant gratification and success may quickly write off Jeremiah as a failure. Yet a careful study reveals him as one of the dominant figures of the Old Testament, outlasting the pomp and power of the kings who marched their armies across the Fertile Crescent. He alone predicted the Israelites' captivity in Babylon would end after seventy years. To him was given a vision to see beyond the horrifying devastation of the moment to God's New Covenant. In the New Testament we find forty-one refer-ences to his prophecies, with significant quotations by Jesus and Paul.

Notable parallels are found between Jeremiah and Jesus. Each was "a man of sorrows, and acquainted with grief." Each experienced rejection and persecution by those they addressed. Some even mistook Jesus for a reincarnated Jeremiah (Matt. 16:14).

Passages with unusual insight to his inner feelings help us to know more about Jeremiah than any of the other prophets. There is no pretense or camouflage in Jeremiah. He gives uninhibited expression to the perplexities and pressures that beset him. One of his most valuable contributions is the revelation of inner struggles, fluctuating moods, and the sometimes startling statements of his feelings toward God.

The name "Jeremiah" literally means "Yahweh hurls." Indeed, when God called Jeremiah, He hurled him into the most tragic and turbulent period of Israel's history. God hurled Jeremiah into the convulsive upheaval of nations of the Near East, as giant empires were rising and falling. During Jeremiah's time one of history's most decisive battles was fought—that of Carchemish in 606 B.C., which made Babylon the dominant world empire and master of the Near East.

Jeremiah had the uncongenial task to prophesy the doom of his nation and the deportation of his countrymen to Babylon. He himself became caught up in the flight of the remnant to Egypt, where tradition has it he was martyred. Only by God's providence has a written record of this chaotic time survived at all.

The Divine Commission

The opening verses twice declare that *The word of the Lord came to him* (1:2, 4). The prophet's message was God's message to the people and to succeeding generations. His prophetic office spanned the last five kings of Judah.

Throughout the Bible we see that God is not stereotyped in His dealings with us. He calls each person in a different manner. *Before I formed you in the womb I knew you, before you were born I set you apart* (v. 5) were God's inaugural words to Jeremiah. This text confirms the sanctity of life in the womb, and makes a powerful statement to the horror of the silent holocaust of over 1.5 million abortions in the U.S. each year.

I appointed you as a prophet to the nations (v. 5) is Jeremiah's daunting commission. "The nations" included, in addition to his own country, the dreaded enemies of Judah to whom he would be a forecaster of doom. True to the meaning of his name, God was hurling Jeremiah into the seething caldron of nations which became instruments of calamity and captivity for the Israelites. To Jeremiah, God's commission would be like an American being told he was appointed a goodwill ambassador to Libya!

The Divine Enablement

Before such a staggering task Jeremiah protests: *I do not know how to speak; I am only a child* (v. 6). In the dialogue of this divine-human encounter, the Lord charges him: *Get yourself ready! Stand up and say to them whatever I command you* (v. 17). Jeremiah is to stand as Athanasius—*contra mundum*—"against the world." He is to *stand against the whole land—against the kings of Judah, its officials, its priests and the people of the land* (v. 18).

But for such an insuperable task comes the divine assurance, *I am with you* (v. 19). With God's commands come His enablements. For each day, God will equip and enable us to do that to which He calls us.

God of Jeremiah, I too feel inadequate for the work You have called me to do. But I thank You that with Your call comes Your enablement.

Broken Cisterns

Read Jeremiah 2:1–8:19

JEREMIAH'S INAUGURAL SERMON, a masterpiece of lyrical lines, depicts a faithless people and a faithful God. The prophet evokes the tender reminiscences of God in the beautiful simile of Israel as His bride: *I remember the devotion of your youth, how as a bride you loved Me and followed Me through the desert* (2:2).

But Israel became ungrateful and unfaithful. God gives an impassioned rebuke for their shameless infidelity (2:5–3:10). The prophet denounces their forsaking God for unholy alliances, and their lack of shame for their sin.

Broken Cisterns

In a memorable passage, the prophet cries out:

> *My people have committed two sins, they have forsaken Me, the spring of living water, and have dug their own cisterns, broken cisterns that cannot hold water* (2:13).

In arid Palestine, a fountain of clear, cool water fed from hidden springs was a rare treasure. To leave a flowing fountain with its sparkling water for the stagnant waters of a cistern was the height of folly. But spiritually that is what the Israelites had done. They had left the purity and holiness of God for the stagnation of moral corruption.

Not only did they "forsake the spring of living water" but they hewed out for themselves broken cisterns of false, worthless gods. It is forever true that when we forsake God, we live by hollow substitutes that do not satisfy the deep thirsts and needs of our life. A hymn writer has expressed it poignantly:

I tried the broken cisterns, Lord,
But, ah! the waters failed;
E'en as I stooped to drink they fled,
And mocked me as I wailed.

RETURN! RETURN! RETURN!

The long-suffering patience and love of God is eloquently expressed in His repeated pleading for Israel to return from her spiritual adultery: *Return, faithless Israel* (3:12); *Return, faithless Israel . . . for I am your husband* (v. 14); *Return, faithless people; I will cure you of backsliding* (v. 22); *O Israel, return to Me* (4:1).

There is impact in Jeremiah's frequent use of repetition. The term "faithless Israel," rendered "backsliding Israel" in the *New King James Version,* is repeated six times in the third chapter. The passage speaks dramatically to us of the peril of going back on God.

God calls the people to repentance, to turn from their idolatry and sin. Then the purified remnant will be restored to fellowship with Him. But they remain obstinate in their rebellion from God and will soon be overtaken by the imminent danger from the north (4:5–6:30) when Babylon shall sweep upon Judah and wreak destruction. The prophet describes the agony of Jerusalem in poignant and graphic terms.

The depravity of the nation was total, so that not one upright person in the nation could be found (5:1-31). They were without shame and, in the prophet's memorable words, *they do not even know how to blush* (6:15; 8:12). It serves a stern warning of the peril of becoming comfortable in sin.

In what is known as Jeremiah's "Temple Sermon" (7:1–8:3) he denounces their ritual as devoid of righteousness and as empty formalism in place of holiness. He gives a blistering denunciation of the people having fallen so far into idolatry that they practiced the abomination of child-sacrifice (7:31). The prophet pronounces the dreaded judgment of God for their obstinacy and gross evils (7:32–8:22).

LORD, FORGIVE MY FORGETFULNESS OF YOU. KEEP ME FROM THE BROKEN CISTERNS OF HOLLOW SUBSTITUTES AND LEAD ME TO THE CLEAR, PURE SPRINGS OF YOUR GRACE.

32

A Balm in Gilead

Read Jeremiah 8:20-22

The Harvest Is Past

Jeremiah, "the master of elegy," laments his people's lost condition: *The harvest is past, the summer is ended, and we are not yet saved* (8:20).

In Palestine the harvest was completed by June, followed by the summer fruit, after which there would be no ingathering. For each soul there may come that awful day when opportunity for salvation is gone and a person who has refused to turn to God becomes forever lost. Death, the great reaper, treads with velvet footfall the path of every life. None can resist that ceaseless mower. We each come to the final harvest as he relentlessly wields his scythe of illness, accident, and violence. Many who plan to be saved at the eleventh hour are visited by the reaper at the tenth.

A Balm in Gilead

Smitten with remorseless grief for his people's incomparable suffering, Jeremiah cries out:

Is there no balm in Gilead? Is there no physician there? Why then is there no healing for the wound of my people? (8:22)

Gilead had long been known for its balm, made from the resin of the mastic tree and used by physicians of the Eastern world. There was "no balm in Gilead" that could cure the Israelites' soul sickness which, because of their obstinacy, was a sickness unto death. In light of the New Testament and Calvary, the piercing pathos of the prophet's question has been answered in the traditional spiritual:

There is a balm in Gilead
To make the wounded whole;
There is a balm in Gilead
To heal the sin-sick soul.

Yes, there is a balm that can heal. Christ came as the Great Physician. He alone can cure the soul of its deadly corruption and give health and life to the one who trusts in Him.

For the believer, in the final harvest of life, the healing balm of Christ turns death into an angel of life. Death becomes the portal of heaven, the vestibule of eternity with our Lord.

GRACIOUS GOD, I PRAISE YOU FOR THE CLEANSING, HEALING, HEALTH, AND WHOLENESS YOU HAVE BROUGHT TO MY LIFE.

33

CAN THE LEOPARD CHANGE HIS SPOTS?

READ JEREMIAH 9–17

SMITTEN WITH HEARTBREAK over Judah's impenitence and imminent doom, Jeremiah cries out: *Oh, that my head were a spring of water and my eyes a fountain of tears! I would weep day and night for the slain of my people* (9:1). It is this lamentation that earned for Jeremiah the title, "the weeping prophet."

His lament is evocative of the One who after him would also climb the pinnacle of pain for His people and cry out: *O Jerusalem, Jerusalem . . . how often I have longed to gather your children together . . . but you were not willing* (Matt. 23:37). God still grieves over those who spurn His love and grace.

THE GRIM REAPER OF DEATH

The prophet, in his lamentation for Jerusalem, paints a graphic picture of death that gives rise to the common figure of the Grim Reaper. Death visits throughout the city, leaving *dead bodies . . . like cut grain behind the reaper* (Jer. 9:22).

Death indeed is the "Grim Reaper" for those outside the

will of God. Our Lord's parable teaches that in the final harvest they will be gathered as weeds to be burned, but the righteous will be as wheat, flourishing forever (Matt. 13:24-30).

An Antidote for Pride

What are the things about which we may boast? Perhaps you are endowed with a keen intellect and impressive education. The prophet warns, *Let not the wise man boast of his wisdom.* Or you may have great energy or physical prowess. The prophet cautions, *Let not . . . the strong man boast of his strength.* Suppose you have everything that money can buy. Jeremiah admonishes, *Let not . . . the rich man boast of his riches.*

Then comes the climax of his homily, *"But let him who boasts boast about this: that he understands and knows Me, that I am the Lord, who exercises kindness, justice and righteousness on earth, for in these I delight," declares the Lord* (Jer. 9:23-24). Indeed, God's grace is the greatest treasure of life, surpassing intellect, power, and wealth. Centuries later the Apostle Paul quotes this very text: *Therefore, as it is written: "Let him who boasts boast in the Lord"* (1 Cor. 1:31).

What does it profit if we have all knowledge, but know not God; have great strength but do not overcome the world; have abundant riches, but forfeit eternal life? If we're going to boast about anything, let it be, as Jeremiah urges, of the Lord's grace and glory in our lives.

From Footrace to Obstacle Course

In Jeremiah's hometown of Anathoth, which had been a sanctuary for him, his own townspeople and family now conspired to take his life (Jer. 11:18-23). He was the forerunner of another who would know the sting of betrayal and the hurt of treachery from among His own.

Jeremiah utters his complaint over the injustice he sees around him. God replies in memorable verse: *If you have raced with men on foot and they have worn you out, how can you compete with horses? If you stumble in safe country, how will you manage in the thickets by the Jordan?* (12:5) God was saying to Jeremiah, "What you have seen so far is only the beginning." The battle was going to get more intense. Jeremiah had been prophesying in the country town of Anathoth. But now he must go to Jerusalem. He had been speaking to his family and friends, but now he must go before priests and kings and nations.

Life often changes from a steady footrace to an obstacle course. The future usually holds more difficulties than we can foresee. We must always be ready for the greater challenges and crises that may come.

Can the Leopard Change His Spots?

In the midst of Jeremiah's further prophecies of the judgment that will strike as drought, famine, and sword, comes one of his most famous texts: *Can the Ethiopian change his skin or the leopard its spots? Neither can you do good who are accustomed to doing evil* (13:23). God declares that when the heart is hardened in pride, sin becomes irreversible. The soul is no longer sensitive to the love and grace of God.

Heart Trouble

The divine cardiologist gives the diagnosis for the doom to come. The spiritual cardiogram of the nation reveals *The heart is deceitful above all things and beyond cure. Who can understand it? I the Lord search the heart* (17:9-10). Sin is a fatal disease of the heart. God alone has the cure. It was provided for all on Calvary.

Lord, with the psalmist of old I pray, "Create in me a clean heart," that I may more worthily love and serve You.

34

The Potter and the Clay

Read Jeremiah 18:1-10

God often uses the commonplace to teach His divine truths. He chose a common scene from Jeremiah's day for a classic parable on His sovereignty.

This is the word that came to Jeremiah from the Lord: "Go down to the potter's house, and there I will give you My message" (18:1). Jeremiah went down as the Lord commanded. He watched the skillful hands of the potter knead the clay and form it into a beautiful vessel. But, before the prophet's eyes, the potter suddenly broke it.

Jeremiah observed that the potter did not discard the clay, but once more took the shapeless mass and kneaded and pummeled and shaped it on his wheel until he fashioned it into an exquisite vessel.

Then the Lord gives His message to the prophet: *O house of Israel, can I not do with you as this potter does? . . . Like clay in the hand of the potter, so are you in My hand* (v. 6).

God, as the Potter, is Sovereign of our lives.

We are the clay. We are the vessel in the making. Clay has no intrinsic worth. It is not valued for itself but for its potential. We are but puny creatures on a pygmy planet that is a speck in the universe. But in the hands of the divine potter we can become a vessel of eternal worth and value.

But the pot he was shaping from the clay was marred in his hands. The potter had a pattern, a design in his mind. Something went wrong. The design miscarried. Perhaps a foreign substance got into the clay.

Something also went wrong with the clay of humanity. An impurity entered into mankind by the Fall of our first parents. God had destined humankind for holy living, but sin marred the design.

So the potter formed it into another pot, shaping it as seemed best to him (v. 4). What an eloquent statement of the indomitable patience of the divine potter who has not cast us aside. At Calvary the pierced hands of the divine craftsman atoned for our flaws and provided a second chance for humankind to be made over again. Praise God, He re-creates the marred vessel! He removes the imperfections and makes it exquisitely beautiful and useful.

The potter is dependent on two natural properties of clay. It has to be pliable—malleable to the whirling wheel, the file, the chisel, and the scorching fire. And it has to be able to be converted by fire. We need to become pliable, yielding ourselves to the skillful hands of the divine potter. Unlike the potter's clay, human clay is given the power to respond. Then, by the converting fire of the Holy Spirit, He will refine and remake us after His own image.

The potter had to break the marred vessel before he could make it over. God has to break us before He can make us. He has to break our stubborn will, crumble our pride, shatter our selfishness, demolish our sin. The process of God's fashioning begins with the difficult step of allowing

Him to break down our resistance and reservations to His will.

The potter beautifies his work with attractive colors and decorative designs. The divine potter dips into His palette and colors and adorns the life with the rich hues of His love, joy, peace, patience, goodness, and strength.

After all the preparation, the pottery is ready to be put to use. It was created, not for itself, but to be put into service, where in Jewish homes vessels of pottery were extremely useful.

Paul, in writing to Timothy, used the image of a potter's vessel to illustrate what God wants to do with our lives: *In a large house there are articles not only of gold and silver, but also of wood and clay; some are for noble purposes and some for ignoble. If a man cleanses himself from the latter, he will be an instrument for noble purposes, made holy, useful to the Master and prepared to do any good work* (2 Tim. 2:20-21).

DIVINE POTTER, HAVE YOUR WAY IN MY LIFE. YOU ARE THE POTTER, I AM THE CLAY. MOLD ME AND MAKE ME ACCORDING TO YOUR WILL.

35

The New Covenant

Read Jeremiah 19–33

Jeremiah gave a blistering denunciation of the impenitent people, their corrupt worship, and the appalling horror that would overtake them. Pashur, chief officer of the temple, upon hearing Jeremiah's baleful prophecy, had him arrested, brutally beaten, and put in stocks (19:14–20:6). Jeremiah paid the high cost of going against the system.

A Burning in My Bones

Jeremiah's honest complaints make him the most human of the Old Testament prophets (20:7-18). He would have preferred not to proclaim the words of doom. However, he acknowledges that God's Word *is in my heart like a burning fire, shut up in my bones* (v. 9).

The caldron described in Jeremiah's early vision is about to spill over in violence from the north. Babylon's mighty army is encamped around Jerusalem, ready to destroy it. Pashur, the king's emissary, now calls Jeremiah for counsel!

Jeremiah was no "health and wealth" preacher. Before Zedekiah, the last of Israel's kings, he forecast not only the doom from the enemy without the walls, but also from the enemy within. The people of Judah had fallen into the hands of an angry God (21:5-7). Jerusalem was going to be destroyed and only those who would surrender to the Babylonians would live (vv. 8-10). The account of the historian Josephus fully supports the details of Jeremiah's role and prophecy, fulfilled in these last days of the Davidic dynasty.

Suddenly a bright ray of sunlight breaks through the ominous clouds of Jeremiah's oracles of doom. Someone is coming! *"The days are coming," declares the Lord, "when I will raise up to David a righteous Branch, a King who will reign wisely and do what is just and right in the land. . . . He will be called: The Lord Our Righteousness"* (23:5-6). This budding Branch—the Messiah—would be a dramatic contrast to the legacy of hopelessness left by those who sat on Judah's throne.

Jeremiah, the country boy who once had run with the footmen, will increasingly contend with the horses! He now moves on to the world scene, from being a voice to Jerusalem to being God's spokesman to the world. He is commissioned to the awesome task of compelling Judah and all the Gentile nations to drink of the wine-cup of the fury of the Lord (25:15-29). His would not be the language of diplomacy but the blunt terms of God's judgment upon them (v. 27). The nations are named in an introduction to the judgments later to be pronounced upon them (chaps. 46–51).

The Restoration

Jeremiah's sermon in the court of the temple enraged the people, who dragged him to trial and demanded the sentence of death, from which he was barely acquitted (26:1-24).

Jeremiah gives the remarkable prophecy that there will

be a return from captivity after seventy years (29:10-14). From out of the storm that rages throughout the book, Jeremiah gives his proclamation of hope (chaps. 30–33): *"There is hope for your future," declares the Lord. "Your children will return to their own land"* (31:17).

The New Covenant

Jeremiah now proclaims the high point, the crown jewel of his prophecies, that of the New Covenant (31:31-34). This text has become the seedbed for distinction between the Old and New Covenants, or the Old and New Testaments. *"The time is coming," declares the Lord, "when I will make a new covenant"* (v. 31). The New Covenant would come to pass in "the fullness of time."

It has a new methodology. The Old Covenant, engraved in stone at Sinai, was external. The New Covenant is internal, engraved on the mind and heart: *I will put My law in their minds and write it on their hearts* (v. 33). *It will be in the words of the Apostle Paul: written not with ink but with the Spirit of the living God, not on tablets of stone but on tablets of human hearts* (2 Cor. 3:3).

The New Covenant results in the forgiveness of sins, when God *will remember their sins no more* (Jer. 31:34).

This charter passage on the New Covenant is quoted at length in Hebrews 8:7-13 to interpret the atoning work of Christ. The New Covenant of which Jeremiah writes is nothing less than the atoning ministry of Christ to each of us.

Jeremiah was not only a prophet of doom, but of deliverance, not only of the exile, but of the restoration, not only of his time, but of the ages.

Covenant God, keep me faithful to the supreme honor of living in covenant with You.

36

God's Invincible Word

Read Jeremiah 36–52

BARUCH THE SCRIBE HAD painstakingly recorded Jeremiah's dictation on a scroll, an expensive parchment of that day. When finished, Baruch, according to Jeremiah's instruction, read the scroll in the temple.

Word of its electrifying contents reached the royal palace. Soon the scroll was summoned to be read to the king. Jehoiakim was sitting in his winter apartment with a fire burning in his brazier in front of him. Whenever three or four columns of the scroll were read the king, with insolent contempt, seized the scroll, cut it off with his knife, and threw it into the fire until the entire scroll was burned.

Seeing their hard work go up in smoke did not stop Jeremiah and Baruch. Jeremiah took another scroll and dictated once more to Baruch, this time adding to its contents (which is probably why his is the longest book of the Bible). The story dramatically illustrates the providence of God in preserving the record of the Old and New Testaments.

Throughout history all attempts to destroy the Word of God have met with defeat.

In the Dungeon of Death

The account next records the series of arrests of Jeremiah, climaxing with him thrown into a cistern. Jeremiah was now advanced in years and no doubt weakened from the effects of the siege, famine, and pestilence that had come to pass. The mire of the deep cistern would suck Jeremiah to a slow but sure death. Again we see the prophet paying a high cost for his faithfulness to the truth (chaps. 37–38).

His rescue is recorded in graphic detail and Jeremiah goes on to prophesy the fall and destruction of Jerusalem and details of history, all remarkably fulfilled (chaps. 39–52).

Lamentations

The Book of Lamentations, with its mournful cry of anguish over the sufferings of Judah and Jerusalem, is an appendage to the Book of Jeremiah. Interspersed in its five dirges are prayers, confessions of sin, calls to repentance, and affirmations of God's grace. Four out of the five chapters are acrostics, each verse beginning in sequence with one of the twenty-two consonants of the Hebrew alphabet.

Jerusalem, destroyed and desolate, is personified as a lonely widow (1:1). Her crown of sorrows is remembering happier days (vv. 6-7). Her plaintive cry longs for sympathy: *Is it nothing to you, all you who pass by? Look around and see. Is any suffering like my suffering?* (v. 12)

In the midst of this incomparable dirge, with its tears and terrors, comes one of the brightest jewels of the Bible: *For His compassions never fail. They are new every morning; great is Your faithfulness* (3:22-23). This textual jewel inspired Thomas Chisholm to write the song that has blessed an innumerable company with the truth of this golden text:

Great is Thy faithfulness, O God my Father,
There is no shadow of turning with Thee;
Thou changest not, Thy compassions they fail not;
As Thou hast been Thou forever wilt be.

Great is Thy faithfulness! Great is Thy faithfulness!
Morning by morning new mercies I see;
All I have needed Thy hand hath provided;
Great is Thy faithfulness, Lord, unto me!

UNCHANGING GOD, I PRAISE AND THANK YOU FOR THE FAITHFULNESS OF YOUR LOVE, YOUR COMPASSION, AND YOUR HOLINESS.

The Multimedia Message

37

God of the Windstorms

Read Ezekiel 1:1-4

Exiles have the unhappiest lot in life. Victims of oppression, war, or political tumult, they are uprooted from their native soil, torn from family and friends, strangers in a strange land. Today the forlorn and tortured faces of these refugees of our world haunt us from the television screens in our living rooms.

Ezekiel was an exile, among the key citizens and families Nebuchadnezzar took to exile in Babylon in 597 B.C., in a region that is now Iraq. Today there is a tomb in Iraq identified as the tomb of Ezekiel. He had been taken from the rustic beauty of the highlands of Jerusalem to the wastelands of Babylon. His brilliant intellect was now employed for a foreign and tyrannous power.

His period coincides with Israel's darkest hour. It was a time of international upheaval, with Israel's monarchy having come to an end. Ezekiel had to proclaim the harsh prophecy of the destruction of Jerusalem and the sacred temple, which took place in 585 B.C., seven years after his call to prophesy.

There were hard questions for Ezekiel to address. The faith of Israel had been linked intimately with the state of Israel and the Promised Land. And now those two foundations were crumbling before them. Had God forgotten them? Was their God inferior to the deities of their enemies who had subdued them?

Yet there in that lonely wasteland God took hold of him and gave him a task and a message that would reach across the centuries. Ezekiel had a twofold message—condemnation and consolation. First he was called to be a prophet of gloom and doom (chaps. 1–32). But his final message was for the restoration of Israel (chaps. 33–39) and of the restored world community (chaps. 40–48).

The Book of Ezekiel has a number of hallmarks. It depicts the grand themes of God's sovereignty, judgment, and mercy in compelling visions, images, oracles, and parables. He acted out his message in prophetic symbolism more than any other prophet. For those who may be fascinated by the weird and the "way out" Ezekiel, with his strange symbolic acts, makes a captivating study. But the serious student of this book discovers that Ezekiel, if unpredictable, was one of the most gifted and effective communicators of God's message.

Unlike the other prophetic books which are largely poetic, most of Ezekiel is prose. Repetitions are among his stock in trade, which have a hammering effect. The phrase "son of Man" is repeated eighty-seven times, in contrast to only one other time in the Old Testament. And no less than sixty-five times he quotes the clause or its equivalent: "Then they will know that I am the Lord," emphasizing God's intention to be acknowledged. Ezekiel's events can be dated with precision as he provides more dates (thirteen) than any other prophet.

Ezekiel is rarely quoted in the New Testament except for the Book of Revelation.

Amid the turmoil and tragedy of the Exile, God comes to

the young Ezekiel in Babylon giving to him one of the most magnificent visions in all of Scripture: *While I was among the exiles by the Kebar River, the heavens were opened and I saw visions of God* (1:1). In his inaugural vision, Ezekiel was overwhelmed with an invasion of divine presence which he describes in vivid imagery.

Ezekiel had a vision in brilliant technicolor of the glory of God. It was a vision of divine transcendence. But he also heard the voice of God speaking to him. That for him was an experience of divine immanence. God is indeed the One who is high and lifted up. But the vision and message of Ezekiel reminds us that He is also the One who stoops to meet and speak with us. He is above us, but He also communicates with us.

The encounter with God, after Ezekiel had been in exile for five years, transformed the young prophet-to-be. His life was never again the same. And so it is with each person who has a personal encounter with God. We can never again be the same.

First, Ezekiel had a vision of the storm: *I looked, and I saw a windstorm coming out of the north—an immense cloud with flashing lightning and surrounded by brilliant light.* God came and spoke to Ezekiel out of the storm. It is reminiscent of the text in Job that records: *Then the Lord spoke to Job out of the storm* (Job 40:6).

It evokes the image of God speaking to Moses out of the burning bush, to Elijah in the stillness of the desert, to David by the wind whistling through the mulberry trees. God breaks in upon our world, surprising us with His presence and word.

God still speaks to His people amid the storms that blow across their lives. Let us look and listen for God in the storms that break upon us. As with Ezekiel, we may find that they may well bring the clearest revelation and word of God to us.

GOD, HELP ME HEAR YOUR MESSAGE IN THE STORMS OF MY LIFE.

38

Stupendous Vision

Read Ezekiel 1:5–2:10

THE SECOND SCENE OF Ezekiel's stupendous vision was the four living creatures. They combined strange attributes of humans, beasts, and heavenly beings with an extraordinary chariot-like vehicle on which was a glorious enthroned being (1:5-14).

The detailed description tells us that they had four faces: the face of a man that is God's crown of creation, of a lion that is king of the beasts, of an ox that is the symbol of strength, and of an eagle that is monarch of creatures of the sky. This scene has its parallel in the Apostle John's vision on the island of Patmos (Rev. 4:7). In the Middle Ages these symbols came to represent the four Gospels.

The third scene centered around the four wheels, with wheels within the wheels, that related the living creatures to the earth and could move in any direction (Ezek. 1:15-21). As the American spiritual goes, "Ezekiel saw dem wheels." It has been suggested that the mobility of the wheels to move in any direction symbolizes God's omnipresence; the awesome size of the wheels, God's omnipotence; the rims "full of eyes," God's omniscience.

The fourth scene in the vision directs the prophet's eyes heavenward to the firmament stretched out as a great canopy (vv. 22-24). The fifth scene and climax of the vision was the throne, representing the presence of God and glowing in golden radiance against a rainbow background (vv. 25-27).

The description of the surpassing grandeur of God's glory exceeds our poverty of language. Ezekiel had to fall back on metaphor and suggestion, employing the word *likeness* or its equivalent in his attempt to describe the vision (v. 28). We are always forced to borrow analogies when we try to speak of God. One writer describes such efforts as "arrows shot at the sun that reach but a fraction of their goal and fall back to earth from where they were sent."

Ezekiel was completely "overwhelmed" (3:15). This was the experience of all in the Bible who had a vision of God's glory. Ezra the devout trembled (Ezra 9:4); Job the eloquent became speechless (Job 40:4-5); Daniel the courageous trembled (Dan. 10:8-11); Saul the arrogant fell off his horse and was blinded by God's glory (Acts 9:4, 8-9); and John the Revelator fell as though dead (Rev. 1:17). Our text records that Ezekiel fell stunned and prostrated before the revealed glory of God (Ezek. 3:23).

Stuart Briscoe comments incisively on this scene in his book on Ezekiel, *Dry Bones*: "The modern mind sees man as awesome and God as tiresome. If God is considered at all, He is viewed from the wrong end of a telescope. . . . Today's God is not the God of Ezekiel who puts men on their faces before Him, but rather a pygmy deity who . . . conveniently adapts to the modern scene" (Wheaton, Ill.: SP Publications, 1977, 18–19).

One of the lessons to be derived from the fact that we cannot really understand this vision is that God is beyond our comprehension. And that is good. For if the finite could comprehend the infinite, then the infinite would be finite.

A "Binocular View" of God

Ezekiel's vision eloquently speaks to us of both the transcendence and immanence of God. Transcendence is God far above us, His existence beyond human experience and the material universe. Before God's transcendence, Ezekiel prostrated himself in the dust.

Immanence is the nearness of God and His involvement with us, His presence throughout the universe. Before God's immanence, Ezekiel heard God's voice above the whirling chariot, calling him to a special task.

We need a "binocular view" of God. We need to perceive His awesome majesty and mighty attributes to know God reverently and realistically. We also need to perceive His immanence, His divine love and presence with us. This balanced view enables us to approach God both with due reverence and in a relationship with Him as our Heavenly Father. As Ezekiel, so we need to know both the God who is above us and the God who is within us.

Transcendent God, I come to You in awe and reverence. Immanent God, I come to You as a child to his father.

39

Our Enablement

Read Ezekiel 2

THE FIRST RECORDED WORDS of God to Ezekiel are, *Son of man, stand up on your feet and I will speak to you* (2:1). God did not want to leave Ezekiel prostrate. He had a work for him to do.

When we come to God in awe and reverence, He calls us to "stand up on our feet" and go forth to do His work. God leads us from reverence to responsibility, from worship to work, from adoration to activity, from devotion to duty, from submission to service.

The newly commissioned prophet testifies, *As He spoke, the Spirit came into me.* The prophet was commissioned for a difficult task—he was going to a "rebellious nation" who would continue to be "obstinate and stubborn." He would need a power beyond himself. The Holy Spirit becomes Ezekiel's enablement.

We also need the enabling presence and power of the Holy Spirit to be what God wants us to be and to do what God wants us to do. The Holy Spirit is the secret of our adequacy for life's needs and challenges. The Holy Spirit transforms us from wishers into warriors, from dreamers into doers, from victims into victors.

In our very busyness for God we can become too often full of overwork rather than overflow. The Holy Spirit empowered life is not a deluxe edition of Christianity to be enjoyed by a privileged few. The presence and power of the Holy Spirit is an inescapable imperative for all who would do God's will and work.

We note that Ezekiel did not say that the Spirit came *unto* him, but rather *the Spirit came into me*. May we, as Ezekiel of old, know the indwelling of the Holy Spirit.

We are told that iron and steel are essentially the same—the only difference being the experience of fire. Yet iron as such is almost useless. The skyscrapers, bridges, steamers, and a thousand more of man's modern achievements have been made possible because iron has been changed into steel.

Man is but the iron of humanity. Not until he has been changed by the fire of the Holy Spirit does he become the steel through whom God can achieve His greatest works.

William Booth found the secret of the baptism of the fire of the Holy Spirit in his work and he penned his prayer for his followers around the world to sing:

> *Thou Christ of burning, cleansing flame, Send the fire! Thy blood-bought gift today we claim, Send the fire! Look down and see this waiting host, Give us the promised Holy Ghost, We want another Pentecost, Send the fire!*
>
> *'Tis fire we want, for fire we plead, Send the fire! The fire will meet our every need, Send the fire! For strength to ever do the right, For grace to conquer in the fight, For power to walk the world in white, Send the fire!*

40

GOD'S SENTRIES

READ EZEKIEL 3

IN THE FIRST RECORDED WORDS of the Lord to Ezekiel, He addresses him by the title that will appear eighty-six more times throughout the book: *son of man* (3:1). Perhaps it was to remind Ezekiel of his own frailty and weakness and need to rely upon God's presence and power.

The Lord commanded: *Eat this scroll; then go and speak to the house of Israel* (v. 1). And still the person called of God must assimilate and internalize His Word, become saturated with divine truth. The imperative for each believer is: *Let the Word of Christ dwell in you richly* (Col. 3:16).

Ezekiel began his mission by going among the captives, saying, *I sat where they sat* (Ezek. 3:15, NKJV). Only when he had sat in their place of woe and weeping as captives was he prepared to bring them God's message.

Centuries later Another who invested new meaning in the title *Son of Man,* came and "sat where they sat." He came for thirty-three years among the captives of sin—

among all of us who were exiled from God—and He experienced our sorrows, our poverty, our testings, our hurts and heartaches. The Apostle Paul wrote of it in immortal lines: *For you know the grace of our Lord Jesus Christ, that though He was rich, yet for your sakes He became poor, so that you through His poverty might become rich* (2 Cor. 8:9).

God's Sentries

Following his seven days of sitting in silence the Lord commissioned Ezekiel to be a watchman (Ezek. 3:17) for the nation. This figure of speech was well-suited to Israel for every city had a watchman. The sentry was a key man in every fortified city. His job was to warn of approaching danger. Life and safety were in the hands of the sentinel.

Is not this a calling of every Christian? Are we not all to be God's sentries, warning others of the danger of the enemy of their soul? Our text speaks to us of the immense importance of sharing the Gospel with those who need to hear it. In our home is a motto placed by one of our daughters, which reads: "We are responsible for one another." We need often to be reminded of that truth. As with Ezekiel, so the Lord holds us responsible for others.

With Charles Wesley, we would pray:

A charge to keep I have, A God to glorify, A never-dying soul to save, And fit it for the sky.

To serve the present age, My calling to fulfil, O may it all my powers engage, To do my Master's will.

Help me to watch and pray, and on Thyself rely, assured if I my trust betray, I shall forever die.

41

MULTIMEDIA MESSAGE

READ EZEKIEL 4–8

STRIKING SYMBOLIC ACTIONS, allegories, riddles, rhythmic dance, and oracles become the vehicles for Ezekiel's message. His ministry commences with four symbolic acts dealing with the siege of Jerusalem. First he is bound and shut up as a captive (3:24-27). Next he constructs a model of the siege of the city with a clay tile and familiar objects (4:1-3). Then he lies on his side bound with cords for over a year (vv. 4-8) with each day representing a year of Israel's troubles. Finally, he prepares to eat during this period a measured amount of food and water that would be the starvation rations of a city under siege (vv. 9-17).

All these actions with visual aids illustrated the coming siege of Jerusalem. These, along with his other bizarre actions, no doubt incurred the mockery and derision of his infuriated hearers whose rebellion and impending fate they symbolized.

After the symbolic enactments of the siege the people must have wondered what this crazy man would do next.

Ezekiel is then directed to take the bizarre action of shaving his head and beard (symbol of a captive) with a sword (symbol of the conqueror). His disposal of the shorn locks symbolized the fate awaiting the people (5:1-17). Standing before them, a strange spectacle with bald head and shaven jaw, he says, "This is Jerusalem." He was telling them that this strange and sheared person they saw, and the scattering of his locks to the four winds, represented the sorry state to which Jerusalem was headed.

Many other dramatic actions illustrated God's coming judgment, culminating with Jerusalem symbolized as a caldron under which God Himself will kindle the fire (24:1-27).

Ezekiel was the most versatile communicator and had the greatest multimedia show in the Bible. No wonder the people said of him, "Is he not a speaker of parables?" (20:49, ASV)

To the Western mind of today, Ezekiel's bizarre actions may seem eccentric. Our theology comes to us filtered through abstract dogmas rather than deeds. But God comes to us concretely in the person of Christ. He died on a felon's cross, rose bodily, ascended literally, and announced that He will return visibly.

Throughout these prophetic chapters of doom is the solemn reminder of two great truths. The first is the curse of sin. God declares through the prophet: *The soul that sins shall die* (18:4, RSV). The second is the cure of salvation. God through Ezekiel declares the poignant and powerful message: *I have been broken* (7:9, ASV). On Calvary God was broken for our sin in that most sublime articulation of His love for humankind.

What incalculable debtors we are to the grace of God. Someone has defined "grace" with the acrostic: God's Riches At Christ's Expense. Let us, in grateful and loving response, follow the God who became broken for us on a crude and cruel cross.

Lord Jesus, I love You—not for hope of heaven nor for fear of hell—but for Your being broken on the cross for me, in Your infinite love and sacrifice as revealed on Calvary.

42

A FOREGLIMPSE OF CALVARY

READ EZEKIEL 9–21

EZEKIEL'S MESSAGE OFFERS A foreglimpse of Calvary in the description of the mark on the foreheads of those who would repent and be saved from God's wrath (9:4-6). The Hebrew word translated *mark* is *taw,* the last letter of the Hebrew alphabet, written in the form of an *X,* a slanting cross. Thus Ezekiel prophesied that the sign of the cross would bring God's deliverance.

John the Revelator described the faithful in heaven as those with Christ's name written on their foreheads with the *X* as the first letter of His name (Rev. 14:1). The cross, for every believer since Calvary, has become our symbol of salvation. Bible scholar H.L. Ellison writes: "This is one of the many examples where Hebrew prophets spoke better than they knew."

In the midst of Ezekiel's ominous prophecies of doom comes a ray of hope. God's great and gracious promise to them is: *I will gather you from the nations and bring you back from the countries where you have been scattered, and I will give you back the land of Israel again* (Ezek. 11:17).

This remarkable prophecy had its fulfillment in stages, starting with the return from Babylon and climaxing with the establishment of the state of Israel in May 1948.

God's promise resonates from Calvary to all of us: *I will give them an undivided heart and put a new spirit in them.... They will be My people, and I will be their God* (vv. 19-20). God is still in the heart transplant business. An uncleansed heart is a fatal condition. For each of us He wants to replace our rebellious heart with one filled with His love and purity.

The preacher-prophet, in a telling parable, gives a beautiful messianic promise of the One who will come from the brokenness of Israel: *I Myself will take a shoot from the very top of a cedar and plant it* (17:22). From the pages of Ezekiel we hear God's plea: *Repent!... Why will you die, O house of Israel? For I take no pleasure in the death of anyone, declares the Sovereign Lord. Repent and live!* (18:30-32) Christ came that we need not die but may live—abundantly and eternally in Him. Let us choose salvation over sin, victory over defeat, life over death.

Charles Haddon Spurgeon, known as the "Prince of Preachers," when asked his method of preaching, replied, "I find a text and then make a beeline to the cross." So many of these texts of the prophets point to Calvary.

We would pray in the words of the poet, Albert Orsborn:

O Love upon a cross impaled,
My contrite heart is drawn to thee;
Are thine the hands my pride has nailed,
And thine the sorrows borne for me?
Are such the wounds my sin decrees?
I fall in shame upon my knees.

Now take thy throne, O Crucified,
And be my love-anointed King!
The weapons of my sinful pride
Are broken by thy suffering.
A captive to love's victories,
I yield, I yield upon my knees.

43

Bridging the Gap

Read Ezekiel 22:30

I *looked for a man among them who would build up the wall and stand before Me in the gap* (22:30) is the call and challenge of God, not only in Ezekiel's time, but in our day as well. This verse speaks to us of the great cleavages caused by sin and the fact that, even in this day of our global village, God uses individuals to stand in those gaps.

Our society and world today is imperiled by great gaps. The holocaust of abortion, the scourge of pornography and AIDS, the disintegration of marriage and family, the perversions of our day—all signal that the moral structures of our society and nation are in need of serious repair.

God calls for men and women who today will bridge the gap, who will rebuild the foundations. Who will stand for God in the gap today? Who will build up the foundations of life, of family, of community, of nation? As someone has asked: "If not you, who? If not now, when?"

Dag Hammarsjköld recorded in his diary, "The road to holiness necessarily passes through the world of action."

There can be no bifurcation of the faith into camps of soul-saving and social action. Evangelism and justice are two coordinate themes of the same Gospel of Christ. We have a whole Gospel for the whole person in the whole world.

The road to righteousness and justice must pass through our world of moral chaos and decay. Christ calls each of His followers to be the salt that will keep the world from pollution, and to be the light that will overcome the darkness.

Webster's definition of the phrase "stand in the gap" is "to expose oneself for the protection of something." Like the disciples of old, Christ calls us to a life of servanthood and sacrifice. He calls us from the world's pursuit of upmanship to "gapmanship." He calls us to become expendable for Him. He calls us to a vulnerable involvement amid the tragedies and the moral morass of our world.

Billy Graham has described his first meeting with Mother Teresa. When he was introduced to her by the American consul, she was ministering to a dying person, holding him in her arms. He waited while she helped him face death. When he died, she prayed quietly, gently lowered him to his bed, and turned to greet Graham. He tells what she shared as her calling: "Mother Teresa looks past the physical features of every needy man, woman, or child and sees the face of Jesus staring up at her through them. In every starving child she feeds, she sees Jesus. Around every sick and frightened woman she cares for, she sees Jesus. Surrounding every lonely, dying man she cradles in her arms is Jesus. When she ministers to anyone she is ministering to her Savior and Lord." Mother Teresa provides a living and loving example of what it means to stand in the gap for God.

LOVING GOD, HELP ME TO BE WILLING TO PAY THE PRICE OF CARING, TO STAND IN THE GAPS OF LIFE FOR YOU.

44

The Delight of Your Eyes

Read Ezekiel 24:15-27

THIS MAJOR SECTION of the Book of Ezekiel closes with the poignant statement from God: *I am about to take away from you the delight of your eyes* (24:15). And in that evening Ezekiel's wife died. God's word and the immediate loss of his beloved was no doubt a great shock to the prophet. The intimacy of their relationship is indicated in the phrase, "the delight of your eyes."

His shock is compounded by God's command not to mourn in the conventional manner, but to keep his grief to himself. His uncustomary behavior symbolized that their sacred and beautiful temple, the symbol of God's presence among them, "the delight of their eyes," would also come to an untimely end. They would be stunned to numbness by the immensity of their loss. Even the prophet's bereavement was used to convey God's message. No part of Ezekiel's life was exempt from his vocation.

God still uses our experiences, especially our sorrows of

life, to speak more eloquently for Him than our words. When the dearest treasures of life are snatched from us, it is then that our lives most eloquently witness to His love and grace.

God never wastes the suffering of His people. Trials produce a deepened sense of His presence and a stronger faith. God brings a golden harvest from the furrows of life that pain has cut. He shines His brightest rays of truth and grace out of the darkness through which we pass. Kagawa stated the noble truth that "the sanctification of suffering is the ultimate art of God." Out of Ezekiel's deep sorrow God spoke one of His most powerful messages to the people.

How unforgettably God has spoken through the paralysis of Joni Eareckson Tada, in giving her a ministry to the handicapped people of the world. And through the suffering in the holocaust of Corrie ten Boom's *The Hiding Place,* which portrays how God brings triumph out of the tragedy of His people. And in the imprisonment and martyrdom of Dietrich Bonhoeffer under Hitler's insane Nazism, God brought forth one of His most powerful statements to the world. And what indelible messages He has given us through the great sacrifices under communist oppression of Salvationists Major Hung Shun Yin and Brigadier Josef Korbel.

As God spoke a memorable message through the death of Ezekiel's beloved, so He speaks a special word of grace to us through the sorrows and sacrifices of life. Should there be taken from us "the delight of our eyes"—some precious treasure of life—let us not miss the light He brings in the dark places.

God of our night seasons, thank You for the light You bring to our darkness and the truth You cause to shine from our trials.

45

The Shepherd and the Judge

Read Ezekiel 25–32

Chapters 25–32 are prophecies against the heathen nations. These writings reveal Ezekiel's international perspective and poetic eloquence.

The prophet's oracles speak powerfully of the sovereignty of God over all peoples. God did not fling this planet off into the universe and set it spinning without His providential care and ongoing governance. He is the God of history and in the end, history becomes His story.

These prophecies serve as a reminder of the omnipotence of God compared to the limited potency of rulers and nations. What was true in Ezekiel's time, of the great empires and cities cited in these chapters, is equally true for the rulers and nations of our time. The "empires" of the United States, of Russia, Britain, and the great cities of New York, Moscow, and London, stand only by the sufferance of God. They are all stamped with temporality.

In Shelley's sonnet, *Ozymandias,* the narrator says that once he met a traveler, presumably from Egypt. In the desert he found the remains of a statue, with two trunkless legs, and near them a broken face, all of silent stone. On the pedestal the traveler had deciphered this inscription:

My name is Ozymandias, King of Kings;
Look on my works, ye mighty, and despair!

Ozymandias had seen himself as one of earth's mighty potentates. But he who had the effrontery to style himself "king of kings" left in the desert sands only those broken pieces of stones.

These oracles of the ancient prophet remind us that true greatness is not in wealth, worldly pomp and power, but in reverence for God, in righteousness and justice.

Ezekiel's melancholy messages to the nations describe an escaped fugitive from Jerusalem bearing an eyewitness account of the tragic news, "The city has fallen!" This announcement confirmed Ezekiel's stern prophecies of the city's impending doom.

The account records that many now came to hear the preaching of Ezekiel. Now instead of being vilified, he was vindicated. Ezekiel was recognized as a bona fide prophet. But his hearers came not as a congregation, but as an audience. To them the prophet's words were entertainment, not spurs to action. They were hearers and not doers of the word.

We see today many who become part of a celebrity or personality cult. But the true result of ministry is to be measured, not by how many followers a popular preacher may have, but how many followers of Christ result from the proclamation.

The account also states that because of the faithfulness of Ezekiel's message and the confirming events, *Then they will know that a prophet has been among them* (33:30-33). When the Word of God is faithfully proclaimed, and the life of the messenger is in accord with its teachings, then in the end people will know that a person of God has been among them.

In chapter 34 Ezekiel, through the pastoral metaphor of the shepherd, conveys the assuring message of God's unfailing love and care for His people. God as the Good Shepherd speaks through the prophet: *I Myself will search for My sheep and look after them. . . . I will rescue them. . . . I will pasture them. . . . I will tend them. . . . I will search for the lost and bring back the strays. I will bind up the injured and strengthen the weak. . . . I will shepherd the flock with justice* (vv. 11-16).

But the compassionate and caring ministry of the divine Shepherd is tempered with justice as He declares: *As for you, My flock, this is what the Sovereign Lord says: I will judge* (v. 17). For each of us who as sheep have gone astray, there will be a day of accountability when the Good Shepherd will also be the Judge of all the earth (vv. 17-22).

This prophecy would have its ultimate fulfillment in Christ, the Good Shepherd: I will place over them one shepherd, *My servant David, and he will tend them; he will tend them and be their shepherd. . . . I will make a covenant of peace with them. . . . There will be showers of blessing* (vv. 23-25).

May our prayer be that of Anna Warner's hymn:

Savior, like a shepherd lead us, Much we need Thy tender care; In Thy pleasant pastures feed us, For our use Thy folds prepare,
Blessed Jesus, Blessed Jesus,
Thou hast bought us, Thine we are.

46

A Heart Transplant

Read Ezekiel 36:1-37

The heart of the problem for rebellious Israel, as well as for all those who are outside of the will of God, is the problem of the heart. In what many consider to be the highest peak of Ezekiel's prophecy, God promises to give a spiritual heart transplant: *I will give you a new heart and put a new spirit in you* (36:26). *He takes away the heart of stone* (v. 26), the heart that has been hardened against His call, and puts in its place a pure and obedient heart.

This promise is for nothing less than the radical transformation of our inner life. The biblical word for "heart" has volitional overtones, not merely emotional ones as in the English. For the Christian, self-will is replaced with a will to serve God.

To be a Christian is to become a new person in Christ. Old things are passed away. Old desires and ways of life give way to a whole new orientation and value system. A popular chorus at the time of my conversion expressed it simply:

Things are different now,
Something happened to me
When I gave my heart to Jesus.
Things are different now,
Something happened that day,
When I gave my heart to Him.
Things I loved before have passed away,
Things I love far more have come to stay.
Things are different now,
Something happened to me,
When I gave my heart to Him!

Praise God, He gives us a new heart. He puts a new spirit within us. He performs the radical surgery that we need to become, in the words of the Apostle Paul, "a new creation in Christ."

God also declares, *And I will put My Spirit in you* (v. 27). This is the secret of the complete change of heart, of the transformation of life in Christ. The Holy Spirit does His creative work within us. He is the agent of our regeneration and our sanctification.

Lyricist George Jackson (1866–93) has expressed our heart's longing in his hymn:

I want, dear Lord, a heart that's true and clean,
A sunlit heart, with not a cloud between;
A heart like Thine, a heart divine,
A heart as white as snow;
On me, dear Lord, a heart like this bestow.

47

AN AMAZING PROPHECY

READ EZEKIEL 36–37

EZEKIEL PRESENTS GOD'S stunning promise of the restoration of Israel: *For I will take you out of the nations; I will gather you from all the countries and bring you back into your own land* (36:24). For Israel it was to be a time of cleansing from their sin and of abundant fruitfulness in their land (vv. 28-38).

The miraculous fulfillment of this promise in our time is one of the great phenomena of history. Never has a nation gone out of existence and returned after a burial of centuries, as has Israel. Twice destroyed as a nation, dragged away as slaves, and having endured centuries of worldwide dispersion and the pogroms of Hitler and Stalin—the odds of survival were formidable beyond reckoning. Yet God prophesied some 2,600 years ago through Ezekiel, *I will bring you back to the land of Israel. . . . I will settle you in your own land* (37:12, 14).

On May 14, 1948 this prophecy was miraculously fulfilled when Israel once again became a nation. Israel's captors, the

Babylonians, along with other great Old Testament nations—Hittites, Philistines, Amalekites, Assyrians—all have disappeared in the sands of time. Because of agricultural technology, the hills and valleys of Israel are fruitful as never before, which also was prophesied by Ezekiel. The prophecies of the Bible are history prewritten, inspired by the foreknowledge of God.

The Vision of the Dry Bones

This text (37:1-14) is perhaps the best known passage of Ezekiel, thanks in part to the popular Negro spiritual taken from it. The prophet is transported by the Spirit to a valley of dry bones scattered over its desert floor.

Looking at the vast number of bones, God asks Ezekiel, *Can these bones live?* What a strange question. How could dry bones live? But Ezekiel had learned enough from his dealings with God to know that the Lord was not prone to ask foolish questions. He knows dry bones can't live, but he answers carefully, *O Sovereign Lord, You alone know.*

Then the Lord said to him, *Prophesy to these bones.* Of all the bizarre things God had told him to do, this was the most preposterous! "What was that again, Lord?" we can hear him say. "I said, 'Prophesy to these bones.' " Perhaps he felt he had been preaching to the dead before, but never as dead as these bleached bones! He had done many eccentric things in his obedience to God but this was absurd. In spite of his incredulity at such a command, Ezekiel starts to preach to the dry bones, declaring that God would restore them to life.

Imagine the spine-tingling surprise as he is preaching, and hears a clanking and a rattling as the bones click into place and become whole skeletons. Then before his awestruck gaze, the skeletons become clothed with muscle and sinew and wrapped in skin. The valley has suddenly become a vast mortuary.

God then tells the prophet to call for the wind or spirit (Hebrew word *ruach* can mean either) to come into the lifeless bodies. And as he did so, *breath entered them; they came to life and stood up on their feet—a vast army* (v. 10). Ezekiel witnessed the phenomenal transformation of a boneyard into a battalion.

The message is then given to the prophet that the dry, bleached bones lying lifeless on the valley floor are the scattered Israelites whom the Lord will ultimately restore to the land of their covenant. For the exiles whose existence was a living death, this was a message of great hope.

We draw an analogy from this dramatic vision. The Valley of Dry Bones can symbolize the human race. We are exiled from God and dead in our trespasses and sins. The proclamation of the prophet has become the proclamation of the Gospel—that the Lord has an abundant and eternal life for those who are born of the Spirit.

HOLY SPIRIT, COME AS THE WIND AND BLOW ACROSS MY LIFE, IMPARTING LIFE, UNITY, AND STRENGTH.

48

"SHOWERS OF BLESSING"

READ EZEKIEL 38–48

I WILL MAKE A COVENANT *of peace with them. . . . There will be showers of blessing* (34:25-26) is God's gracious promise to Israel. Ezekiel's prophecy and words inspired James McGranahan's familiar hymn, which may well serve as our prayer response to this text:

> *There shall be showers of blessing, Send them upon us, O Lord,*
> *Grant to us now a refreshing. Come and now honor Thy Word.*
> *There shall be showers of blessing, O, that today they might fall,*
> *Now as to God we're confessing, Now as on Jesus we call.*

GOG AND MAGOG

The final chapters dealing with Gog and Magog (chaps. 38–39) and the new temple with its tedious details of measurements and regulations (chaps. 40–46) are beyond our clear understanding. They have been subject to what Adam Clarke calls "an ocean of conjecture." Commentators and exegetes agree that these are among the most difficult of Old Testament passages. Thus this writing will not repeat nor add to the "hermeneutical alchemy" that surrounds these chapters. Nonetheless there are central truths to be gleaned from these writings of Ezekiel.

Gog is symbolic of all the evil powers and the enmity of this world which will one day be arrayed against God's people and destroyed by God's intervention. In the Book of Revelation Gog appears again as the ungodly world power, led by Satan, which perishes in final conflict with God's people (Rev. 20:7-10). The central truth revealed is that God will ultimately destroy the evil powers of this world.

The River of Life

Appropriately, Ezekiel's prophecies and visions close with that of the ever-increasing stream of redemption and the city of God (chaps. 47–48). His visions climax with the blessings of those who serve the Lord in the new kingdom of God where there flows the river of the water of life.

The prophet's final vision of the life-giving river calls to mind the words of Jesus, *If a man is thirsty, let him come to Me and drink. Whoever believes in Me, as the Scripture has said, streams of living water will flow from within him* (John 7:38). John the Revelator describes also the "river of the water of life" that flows in the eternal kingdom of God (Rev. 22:1).

Ezekiel concludes his record of remarkable visions with that of the city of God. It is a city of perfect architectural proportions, symmetrical design, free access, and has a healing and life-giving stream. But its crowning glory will be the presence of God in its midst. The final and culminating words of this magnificent book is the name of the city, which interpreted is, *The Lord Is There.*

The crowning quality of any place or work or life is just that—the very presence of God. Through the grace of our Lord Jesus Christ and the ministry of the Holy Spirit, that can be our glorious day-by-day experience.

Let us drink of that life-giving stream of redemption, with the words of the late General Albert Orsborn as our prayer:

When shall I come unto the healing waters?
Lifting my heart, I cry to thee my prayer.
Spirit of peace, my Comforter and healer,
In whom my springs are found,
Let my soul meet thee there.

From a hill I know,
Healing waters flow;
O rise, Immanuel's tide,
And my soul overflow!

Wash from my hands the dust of earthly striving;
Take from my mind the stress of secret fear;
Cleanse thou the wounds from all but thee far hidden.
And when the waters flow let my healing appear.

Light, life and love are in that healing fountain,
All I require to cleanse me and restore;
Flow through my soul, redeem its desert places,
And make a garden there for the Lord I adore.

The Crown Jewels of Prophecy

49

God's Perfect Prophet

Read Daniel 1

THE STARTLING AND THRILLING stories of the Book of Daniel have held a fascination for many of us from our childhood days. Who does not know the enthralling accounts of a captive young Hebrew, of mighty King Nebuchadnezzar, of Belshazzar's impious feast and his awful doom, of the three children in the fiery furnace and Daniel in the lions' den. Truth is indeed stranger and more wonderful than fiction. No Arabian Nights' Entertainments can compare with the captivating stories of Daniel.

And what serious student of Scripture has not been detained by the sublime visions of Daniel and his mysterious and majestic prophetical teachings?

We know more about Daniel than any of the other prophets. He was of the tribe of Judah, of noble and possibly royal blood, and was carried captive from Jerusalem to Babylon in 606 B.C. when in his late teens. In a short time he rose to a very high position in the empire and lived through the whole period of the "Seventy Years Captivity."

Daniel is the only spotless character in the Bible outside of Christ. There is not a flaw to be found in his character. Daniel is referred to in the great faith chapter as the one who "stopped mouths of lions" (Heb. 11:33). He personified a life of faithfulness, prayer, and obedience. His daily contacts with international politics give his writings an extra quality of practicality. He led a public life, associating with kings and politicians. He held political office, yet his character was never impeached. He talked with angels. The Lord Himself appeared to him and he had visions of God.

Daniel lived during an age of tremendous international upheaval. Nebuchadnezzar, military and political genius, brought the Babylonian Empire to its zenith of power, wealth, and world leadership. It was a time when ancient empires were vanishing and a new empire was on the horizon. Daniel's own people were passing through their dark night of trial, exiled from their homeland of promise, servants in a pagan land. They hung their harps on the willows and hoped for the dawning of a new day.

Authentic Authorship

Perhaps no other book of the Bible has been attacked as much by critics as the Book of Daniel. For 1,600 years it has been in the "Critic's Den."

Ezekiel, a contemporary of Daniel, twice mentions Daniel as deserving to be ranked with Noah and Job (14:14), and he is renowned for his wisdom (28:3).

On the Tuesday before His crucifixion, Jesus gathered His disciples with Him on the Mount of Olives and talked to them about the end of the world. During this "Olivet Discourse," Jesus referred to statements of Daniel almost 600 years earlier. In doing so, He referred to him as "the Prophet Daniel" (Matt. 24:15). Our Lord Himself endorsed both the genuineness of his message and the validity of Daniel as prophet.

The Apostle Paul also refers to Daniel in 2 Thessalonians 2:3-4. The fact that the Book of Revelation quotes from Daniel more than any other Old Testament book is further confirmation of its status in the Bible. The Book of Daniel is also found in the Septuagint, completed in 285 B.C. It includes references made by Josephus, the Jewish historian who writes of the incidents in the struggle with Antiochus Epiphanes: "according to the prophecy of Daniel which was given 408 years before." This writing of Josephus would place the Book of Daniel around 573 B.C. Josephus also relates that when Alexander the Great came to conquer Jerusalem in 332 B.C., Jaddua, the high priest, showed Alexander the reference to passages prophesying his rise to power in the Book of Daniel (Dan. 8:5-8). This so pleased Alexander that he spared the city.

The inspiration of this great book is attested by history, the Bible itself, and the unimpeachable testimony of our Lord.

Reader, Bible student, seeker of eternal truth, get ready for a magnificent adventure in one of the greatest books of God's Word!

GOD OF DANIEL, OPEN THE EYES OF MY HEART AND MIND TO GRASP THE SUBLIME TRUTHS OF THIS MAGNIFICENT BOOK YOU HAVE GIVEN US.

50

"Purposed in His Heart"

Read Daniel 1:1-8

THE OPENING CHAPTER gives us a vivid portrait of Daniel, and its dramatic encounter sets the tone for the rest of the book. It presents Daniel, a brilliant young man of noble or royal blood, a citizen of a conquered race, and a member of an ethnic minority who faces a severe test of his loyalty to God.

Prophecy Fulfilled

The opening verses of this book are a dramatic fulfillment of divine prophecy. Nebuchadnezzar, king of Babylon, conquers Judah, pillages the temple, and carries away select youth from the royal family to serve in the king's palace. This Babylonian Captivity was predicted in detail over a century earlier by the Prophet Isaiah: *The time will surely come when everything in your palace, and all your fathers have stored up until this day, will be carried off to Babylon. Nothing will be left, says the Lord. And some of your descendants, your own flesh and blood who will be born to you, will be taken away, and they will become eunuchs in the palace of the king of Babylon* (Isa. 39:6-7). The Prophet Jeremiah also predicted this Captivity (Jer. 25:8-12).

Captive in a Strange Land

The king wanted the finest young men for service in his house and royal court. Our text describes those who were selected: *from the royal family and nobility—young men without any physical defect, handsome, showing aptitude for every kind of learning, well informed, quick to understand, and qualified to serve in the king's palace* (Dan. 1:3-4).

They would be taught in *the language and literature of the Babylonians.* The Babylonians were notably advanced in mathematics, astronomy, and architecture, as well as involved in divination, magic, a form of astrology, and pagan mythology.

The whole process was designed to "brainwash" them and fully acculturate them into the Babylonian system. This is further evidenced in the changing of the names of Daniel and his three friends. Each of their original given names contained some form of the name of their God, Jehovah, whereas their new names were reminders of the gods of the Chaldeans. This was intended to obliterate any reference to the true God of Israel and keep before them a continuous reminder of the pagan gods of Babylon.

Taken to a captive land, separated from family and the support system of his faith, even his God-honoring name changed in homage to a pagan god—everything seemed conspired against Daniel's faithfulness to his God. However, the record declares: *But Daniel resolved . . . not to defile himself* (v. 8).

His courage and resolve have been sung about by many of us in our Sunday School days in the words penned by Philip Bliss:

Standing by a purpose true,
Heeding God's Command,
Honor them, the faithful few;
All hail to Daniel's band!

Dare to be a Daniel,
Dare to stand alone,
Dare to have a purpose firm,
Dare to make it known.

Many mighty men are lost,
Daring not to stand,
Who for God had been a host
By joining Daniel's band.

Many giants, great and tall,
Stalking through the land,
Headlong to the earth would fall
If met by Daniel's band.

Hold the gospel banner high;
On to victory grand;
Satan and his host defy
And shout for Daniel's band.

ETERNAL GOD, GIVE ME COURAGE TO BE FAITHFUL WHEN IN THE MIDST OF A CULTURE THAT IS UNKNOWING OR HOSTILE TOWARD YOU.

51

TESTED IN A STRANGE LAND

READ DANIEL 1:8-21

THERE CAME A VERY EARLY test to Daniel and his young Hebrew companions serving in the king's court. *The king assigned them a daily amount of food and wine from the king's table* (1:5). Such food would have first been dedicated to a heathen god in sacrifice. Sharing in it would mean honoring the god to which it had been offered. In response we have one of the great verses that delineates Daniel's character: *But Daniel resolved not to defile himself with the royal food and wine* (v. 8).

Daniel gives evidence that early godly training nurtures deep roots of character. They could carry him away from his homeland, his sanctuary of faith, and all that had been held dear, but they could not separate him from the influence of his early godly training. His faith was further strengthened by prayer and the Scriptures to guide him in this crucial time.

Daniel asked for a "religious exemption" from partaking of the royal food. This was not granted. The official replied, *Why should he [the king] see you looking worse than the other young men your age? The king would then have my head because of you* (v. 10).

Daniel's Diet

With exquisite courtesy, Daniel then asked for a test: *Please test your servants for ten days: Give us nothing but vegetables to eat and water to drink. Then compare our appearance with that of the young men who eat the royal food, and treat your servants in accordance with what you see* (vv. 12-13). The results: *At the end of the ten days they looked healthier and better nourished than any of the young men who ate the royal food* (v. 15). Their request for exemption was now granted.

The record states that after the ten-day test, Daniel and his three friends "looked healthier and better nourished [KJV mistakenly translates this word as 'fatter'] than any of the young men who ate the royal food." They were vegetarians. Vegetarianism is not something new in this diet fad generation. But his is the first generation in history to document its virtues and benefits. To shun the king's rich food and meats must have seemed foolish to their peers, but Daniel and his three Hebrew friends had a wisdom that our age is just beginning to discover.

When the period of their three years' training was completed, the king himself examined those that had been selected for his service. The Scripture account tells us *he found none equal to Daniel* [and his friends] . . . *in every matter of wisdom and understanding about which the king questioned them, he found them ten times better than all the magicians and enchanters in his whole kingdom* (vv. 19-20).

Our "Oriental Court"

Daniel and his friends had been carried away into a strange land. Do we not find life often does that to each of us? We too are carried away into a new situation and place. The stability of the way of life that we knew with our loved ones has disappeared. The march of time in each life brings us to face the unknown, untried and uncertain.

Someone has suggested that in our era "we have been carried away by our science into a wonderful oriental court, but one that is full of danger." The simple life of our forebears seems very remote to us and we are caught up in the "luxurious life of Babylon."

There is that moment for many young people when they go from the threshold of their home, with all its support and security, out into the maelstrom of the world. They are suddenly cut loose from the protective moorings they have known and need the anchor of faith that has been nurtured in godly training and will be strengthened by sacred memories. They face new temptations and testings. They will be tempted to indulge and forget the lessons of early virtue, to abandon the principles in which they have been trained.

Perhaps each life finds itself in a succession of experiences of being "carried away" far from the familiar landmarks and safe boundaries. We are all pilgrims on life's journey. As we face the new frontier of such major changes as school, marriage, and career, we will be confronted with great challenges to our character and faith. But we, like Daniel, if we "purpose in our heart not to defile ourselves," will grow and be strengthened amid life's testings. There is security and strengthening of character for the man and woman who have an abiding loyalty to God.

HOLY GOD, ESTABLISH IN ME THE FOUNDATIONS OF FAITH THAT WILL STAND THE TESTING TIMES, THAT I, AS DANIEL, WILL STAND "BY A PURPOSE FIRM."

52

Tested by Fire

Read Daniel 3:1-23

Its construction and technology must have been the topic of conversation for months. The colossus made by Nebuchadnezzar was ninety feet high and nine feet wide and could be seen for miles. The building of this image can also be construed as an act of the emperor's self-deification. It surely was the talk of the empire!

Dedication of the Image

The dedication of the golden image was an elaborate affair. An executive order went forth that summoned all the leaders of the provinces.

You cannot have a dedication without music. An elaborate orchestra had been assembled and had months of rehearsals. The orchestra had a vital part in the dedication, for the king's herald *loudly proclaimed . . . as soon as you hear the sound of the horn, flute, zither, lyre, harp, pipes and all kinds of music, you must fall down and worship the image of gold that King Nebuchadnezzar has set up* (3:4-5). The stern demand was proclaimed throughout the kingdom so that everyone knew that when the symphonic sound was heard, it was the cue to prostrate themselves before the golden image and pay homage to the king.

To forestall any rebellion, the king constructed a large furnace within sight of the image and in his decree warned: *Whoever does not fall down and worship will immediately be thrown into a blazing furnace* (v. 6).

The Faithful Three

The orchestra struck the note, and as its symphonic sounds wafted across the plain, *All the peoples, nations and men of every language fell down and worshiped the image of gold that King Nebuchadnezzar had set up* (v. 7).

"All the peoples," except for the three devout friends of Daniel—Shadrach, Meshach, and Abednego. The astrologers were quick to report to the king the defiance of the faithful three.

The monarch became "furious with rage" and summoned the three Hebrews. How dare they defy his edict. How dare they not pay homage to his gods. Had he not promoted these slaves to positions of great honor?

The furious king gave them one more chance to repent and worship his god. In his fury, he warned them: *But if you do not worship it, you will be thrown immediately into a blazing furnace. Then what god will be able to rescue you from my hand?* (v. 15)

With courage and calmness, the faithful three answered: *If we are thrown into the blazing furnace, the God we serve is able to save us from it. . . . But even if He does not, we want you to know, O king, that we will not serve your gods or worship the image of gold you have set up* (v. 18). The word "if" is all important. They were not questioning God's ability, but were prepared to accept His will should God not intervene.

History is replete with those who kept the faith even when the flames consumed—Stephen praying as his battered body became covered with a mound of stones; Polycarp keeping the faith amid the flames at the stake; Bonhoeffer believing as he went to the gallows.

The three Hebrews acknowledged they had no claim on divine intervention, but had absolute faith in God's almighty power. Their "if" is reminiscent of Job's testimony: "Though He slay me, yet will I trust Him"; and Jesus' words in the garden, "Nevertheless, not Mine but Thy will be done."

The response of the faithful three served only to increase the rage of the king who ordered his furnace to be made seven times hotter. The fire stoked to its sevenfold heat scorches to death the executioners who had bound the Hebrews and pushed them into the furnace. The record states of the faithful three: *and these three men, firmly tied, fell into the blazing furnace* (v. 23).

Our faith may well be tested by fire. Circumstances may take hold of us and put us through a fiery test and trial. If it does, may we, as the three faithful servants of old, say, "Our God is able!"

ALMIGHTY GOD, WHEN CIRCUMSTANCES OVERTAKE AND WOULD OVERWHELM ME, HELP ME NOT TO TAKE THE EASY WAY OUT, BUT TO BE FAITHFUL IN THE HOUR THAT TRIES BY FIRE.

53

FIREPROOF FAITH

READ DANIEL 3:23-30

THE KING HAD A "ringside seat" to the drama. The three faithful Hebrews, firmly tied, had been pushed into the blazing furnace that had been stoked to a sevenfold heat and had scorched to death the executioners. But as the king watches he is suddenly filled with amazement and asks his advisers if there were not *three men that we tied up and threw into the fire?* (3:24) With their assuring response, he exclaims, *Look! I see four men walking around in the fire, unbound and unharmed, and the fourth looks like a son of the gods* (v. 25).

The king himself approaches the opening of the blazing furnace and shouts for the three men to come out, addressing them as "servants of the Most High God." The king's cabinet and high officials looked on in astonishment as they saw *that the fire had not harmed their bodies, nor was a hair of their head singed; their robes were not scorched, and there was no smell of fire on them* (v. 27).

Many commentators believe that the fourth person in

the fiery furnace was a theophanic appearance of the Son of God, a preincarnate manifestation of Christ. We are reminded of the comforting truth that we do not face life's tests and trials alone, but His presence is ever with us. Centuries ago, Isaiah gave us the beautiful promise:

> *When you pass through the waters I will be with you; and when you pass through the rivers, They will not sweep over you. When you walk through the fire, you will not be burned; the flames will not set you ablaze* (Isa. 43:2).

The faith of these three men becomes enshrined in that Westminster Abbey of the Bible, Hebrews 11, with its roll call of heroes "who through faith . . . quenched the fury of the flame" (Heb. 11:33-34).

King Nebuchadnezzar was constrained to issue a decree: *Praise be to the God of Shadrach, Meshach and Abednego, who has sent His angel and rescued His servants! They . . . were willing to give up their lives rather than serve or worship any god except their own God* (v. 28). The king decreed his sovereign protection of the faithful three and promoted them in the kingdom.

"Our God Is Able"

The external setting may be different, but the inner truth of this great chapter abides. There are still many who know the experience of a fiery furnace, of a brutal force that seeks to destroy faith, and a Presence that enables them to survive the testing by fire.

The setting of this Scripture is no more barbaric than our own time. The distance from Nebuchadnezzar's furnace to the fiery furnaces of the Holocaust is not that great. And what about the "silent holocaust" with the 1.5 million legalized abortions every year in our country?

This chapter may be as up to date as any in the Bible. Even as we study it, devout Christians in certain countries of the world are suffering in prison for their faith, some even facing death. Millions are oppressed, imprisoned, and put to death for their faith in our own day. Some Christian leaders have stated that there have been more martyrs for the faith in our time than in all previous history.

And it will get worse. The last book of the Bible tells us that in the end time the whole world will come under the persecution of a system called Babylon. Idolatrous worship of a symbolic image will be enforced upon all. Death will be the penalty of nonconformity (Rev. 13).

This great text in Daniel reminds and encourages us that "our God is able." Our faith can persevere and survive the fieriest tests. When we go through the fiery furnace experience, we will find One who will be with us and will make us adequate.

STRONG DELIVERER, GIVE ME A FIREPROOF FAITH.

54

THE MAN WHO HAD EVERYTHING

READ DANIEL 4:1-9

THIS CHAPTER IS AUTOBIOGRAPHICAL, related by the infamous King Nebuchadnezzar. One expositor calls it, "his own account of his conversion."

THE KING'S PROCLAMATION

This chapter has rightly been described as one of the most remarkable "state documents" ever to come down to us from ancient times. It was a proclamation of King Nebuchadnezzar to the whole world, in 562 B.C., the year he recovered from his insanity, and one year before his death. It is a confession of sin, an explanation of his insanity, and his testimony of conversion.

His edict is proclaimed universally: *To the peoples, nations and men of every language, who live in all the world.*

The proclamation begins almost as one would give their witness to God's work in their life today: *It is my pleasure to tell you about the miraculous signs and wonders that the Most High God has performed for me.*

The king rhapsodizes: *How great are His signs, how mighty His wonders! His kingdom is an eternal kingdom; His dominion endures from generation to generation.*

The witness of Daniel and his friends must have had a great impact on the king. He had seen the young men refuse to eat his royal food and then, after their test, be the most wholesome in appearance in all his court. He had experienced Daniel's extraordinary interpretation of his dream, when all his astrologers and magicians had failed. He had witnessed the astonishing miracle of the deliverance of Daniel's three friends from his fiery furnace and the presence of "one like the Son of God" in the furnace with them. Daniel's exemplary faith and life no doubt was well known to the king. Thus it is possible that Daniel, the only major personage in the Bible other than Christ Himself whose life had no recorded flaw, was instrumental in this renowned king coming to know God and His salvation in his own life.

It is noteworthy that the king addresses Daniel by his Hebrew name. Before the king's conversion, he addressed Daniel as Belteshazzar, which was his Chaldean name after the Chaldean god. But the name Daniel in Hebrew symbolized Daniel's faith, for it meant "God is my Judge." This is an acknowledgment of homage to Daniel's God, the true and living God.

The King's Pride

We hear the king describing himself as basking in his royalty: *I, Nebuchadnezzar, was at home in my palace, contented and prosperous* (4:4). "Contented and prosperous"—a portrait of the man who had everything. Contentment and prosperity are still the primary goals of many people today.

Nebuchadnezzar had reached the pinnacle of achievement. His kingdom was flourishing. In his mood of self-gratification he admired the splendors of his achievements.

His royal palace was without parallel, adorned in gold and brilliant colors of glazed tile. He had built one of the seven wonders of the ancient world—the Hanging Gardens he had made for his queen. Walls encompassed the city and chariot teams could race abreast for 130 miles upon their top. One hundred gateways, with brass gates, controlled access to the city. A great reservoir, 138 miles in circumference, conserved and controlled the waters of the Euphrates River. Canals were built for navigation and irrigation and his breakwater made the Persian Gulf safe for Babylonian boats. What could possibly intrude upon such prosperity and contentment?

Our Western culture is plagued by the passion to possess. Our lust for affluence borders on the psychotic. We need to hear and heed the advice of Corrie ten Boom who endured the brutality of a Nazi prison camp during World War II. She said that she had learned to hold everything loosely for she discovered that when she grasped things tightly, it would hurt when the Lord would have to pry her fingers loose. Christian disciples learn to hold all things loosely.

HEAVENLY FATHER, SAVE ME FROM COMPULSIVE EXTRAVAGANCE AND TEACH ME THE DISCIPLINE AND VIRTUE OF SIMPLICITY.

55

A King's Disturbing Dream

Read Daniel 4:10-37

The King's Perplexity

King Nebuchadnezzar had a disturbing dream. It haunted him and became an unwelcome intruder upon his contentment. He summoned before him all his magicians, enchanters, astrologers, and diviners. But none of them could interpret his dream for him.

In final desperation, he called Daniel, affirming that no mystery was too great for Daniel's God to reveal. He related the dream of a tree that grew to enormous height, *visible to the ends of the earth. Its leaves were beautiful, its fruit abundant, and on it was food for all* (4:12). But then a "watcher" appeared, who ordered the tree to be cut down and destroyed, with only its stump standing, in the grass of the field.

The watcher continued: *Let him be drenched with the dew of heaven, and let him live with the animals among the plants of the earth. Let his mind be changed from that of a man and let him be given the mind of an animal, till seven times pass by for him* (vv. 15-16).

Daniel's Prophecy

Daniel knew well the meaning of the dream, but was hesitant to tell the king its horrifying interpretation. Encouraged by the king, Daniel gave its meaning. *You, O king, are that tree! You have become great and strong; your greatness has grown until it reaches the sky, and your dominion extends to distant parts of the earth* (v. 22). Then Daniel had to tell the king that if he would not change his ways, he would become irrational, living and eating like an animal. Daniel told the king that he would remain in this condition until "seven times," or seven years.

The king failed to heed Daniel's advice to "renounce your sins by doing what is right."

The King's Plight

As the king was walking about on the roof of his majestic palace, overlooking his magnificent gardens, suddenly a bizarre metamorphosis took place. The proud king fell down and started to creep on all fours, destined to live like an animal for the next seven years.

The king's insanity, lycanthropy, was fairly common centuries ago when people lived closer to animals. The once proud king lived with his hair uncombed, matted until it grew together like the feathers of an eagle, his fingernails grew coarse and long until they became like the claws of an eagle, and he lived like a wild animal in the grass of the field. But he would survive and after seven years was restored to his right mind and his kingdom.

The King's Penitence

Upon his restoration, the king showed a great change of heart. This has been interpreted by some expositors as an experience of repentance and conversion. The king testified: *I, Nebuchadnezzar, raised my eyes toward heaven, and my sanity was restored. Then I praised the Most High; I honored and glorified Him who lives forever* (v. 34). The king goes on to extol the sovereignty of God. It is an extraordinary story and statement from the royal court of this great king of an ancient empire.

God's Power

This story from ancient times has lessons that are always contemporary. It preaches a powerful message on the sovereignty of God. One of the key phrases in this chapter is "the Most High," found three times. This text reminds us that all of the kingdoms and powers of men are under the sovereignty of God and in subjection to His ultimate will and working in the course of history.

Sovereign God, save us from the poison of self-absorption and self-seeking and lead us to an acknowledgment of Your lordship over us and the world.

56

THE KING'S BANQUET OF DEATH

READ DANIEL 5

THE KING'S FEAST

A ROYAL BANQUET TONIGHT at the king's palace! A thousand lords and their ladies dressed in regal splendor dismount from their upholstered chariots. There is the glitter of jewels and the rustle of silk mingled with drunken laughter and obscene song. The menu tonight is wine, women, and song. Eat, drink, and be merry!

We hear the recurring refrain through the din of the night, "Long live King Belshazzar," as again and again cups are hoisted and emptied in the orgy of drunkenness and debauchery.

THE KING'S FRIGHT

What is that on the wall? What did they put in that wine? Look—fingers of a hand writing on the wall! Is it a hallucination? Is this a prank being played by the king's revelry makers? Is it a phantom? Over 2,000 eyes are riveted upon the wall. My God, what is it? There is a thousand-voice shriek of horror!

The king is the most shaken of all. His face is blanched, his lips tremble, his knees knock. Never has a drunken man sobered so quickly. Only a few moments earlier this proud monarch had dared to defy God.

When Belshazzar finally found his voice, he began to shout frantically for his experts to explain this mystery. He promised the highest rewards—to be clothed in scarlet with a golden chain around the neck and be promoted to third place in the kingdom. But none of the king's wise men could tell the king its meaning. *So King Belshazzar became even more terrified and his face grew more pale. His nobles were baffled* (5:9).

The Queen Mother comes to the rescue. She reminds the king that in his kingdom is a man *who has the spirit of the holy gods in him* and who had *knowledge and understanding, and also the ability to interpret dreams, explain riddles and solve difficult problems* (vv. 11-12). She said, "Call for Daniel, and he will tell you what the writing means." And so Daniel, long neglected and all but forgotten, now becomes God's man of the hour.

The King's Finish

Daniel is brought into the banquet hall. What a striking figure in contrast as he stands before that drunken crowd. Now, about eighty-eight years of age, courage and confidence radiated from his godly face. The king in essence says, "So you are Daniel!" reiterating what the Queen Mother had said about Daniel. He offers to Daniel great honor and gifts if he would interpret the writing on the wall. But Daniel brushes aside the baubles and goes straight to the crisis facing the drunken king and his empire. He omits the customary salutation, "O King, live forever!" It seemed pointless to Belshazzar.

Daniel courteously but forthrightly gives the king the message from God. He recalls the lessons of history that Belshazzar failed to learn from his grandfather, Nebuchadnezzar, and God's dealings with him. Daniel charges: *But you his son, O*

Belshazzar, have not humbled yourself, though you knew all this. Instead, you have set yourself up against the Lord of heaven (vv. 22-23).

Daniel then gives the interpretation of the handwriting on the wall. *"Mene*—God has numbered the days of your reign and brought it to an end. *Tekel*—You have been weighed on the scales and found wanting. *Peres*—Your kingdom is divided and given to the Medes and Persians."

Meanwhile, the Persians, who for two years had been laying siege to the city, took advantage of the drunken carousal and stormed in. There is the sound of the rushing feet of the conquerors at the palace door and on the palace stair. Death burst upon that banquet scene, darting in with a thousand gleaming knives. The night ends with nothing but torn banners, the slush of spilled over wine, the blood of murdered lords and their ladies, and the kicked and tumbled carcass of a dead king. "That very night Belshazzar, king of the Babylonians, was slain."

The King's Folly

Belshazzar had felt secure. His drawbridges were drawn up, his brazen gates barred, his soldiers on their lofty walls could repulse any attempt to enter by force. The storehouses bulged with food. The Euphrates flowed with water. The city of Babylon was impregnable.

Belshazzar led his drunken lords and ladies in an act of contemptuous sacrilege as they drank wine from consecrated vessels and paid homage to the pagan gods. That became the fatal moment, the turning point of the banquet, turning their glee into gloom, their drunkenness into disaster, their desecration into destruction.

Good Lord, keep me from sins that lead to death.

57

THE TWO BANQUETS

READ DANIEL 5

HISTORY PROPHESIED

TWO ANCIENT HISTORIANS, Herodotus and Xenophon, inform us of the strategy of Cyrus who conquered Babylon. Cyrus had his soldiers divert the water of the river that ran through the city. As Belshazzar feasted in drunken revelry, Cyrus marched his soldiers through the channel of the river, both where it entered and left the city, until they met in the center of the city where the palace was located. The soldiers of Cyrus quickly took possession of the city, stormed the palace, and slew the king.

It is instructive to note that Isaiah had prophesied the fall of Babylon, the very name of its captor, and the manner of its capture, 175 years before the event took place (Isa. 44:28–45:4).

SIN'S BANQUET

The lessons of this ancient story are always contemporary. Belshazzar knew there was a God in Israel. The fiery furnace experience told him so. The mental derangement of his grandfather Nebuchadnezzar told him so. The life of Daniel told him so.

We also have been confronted by evidences of God. Personal experiences have told us there is a God. Great revivals in our time have told us so. Our conscience and the working of God's Spirit in our heart tells us so.

Belshazzar did not forsake his sin. He lived in revelry and worldly attachments. He worshiped false gods. He profaned that which was sacred. We too have allowed our Sabbath to become secularized, our holy days of Easter and Christmas to become commercialized.

We learned also from this story that when God communicates His message to us, we had better read and heed it. Sometimes the writing is by the fingers of sickness, of death, of bereavement, or of the Spirit's wooing. God is still writing His messages for us to read.

The sudden terror of the king who a minute before had been so brazenly confident, reminds us that an hour is coming when every sinner will tremble before God's Judgment Seat.

Daniel was not invited to the great banquet feast. But when crisis came, he was summoned. The person of God often is not sought in prosperity. But when the hour of trouble comes, He is sent for. The call is heard, "Pray for me."

Sin has spread a great banquet in the earth today. It invites all to come and feast at its table. But there is a dramatic difference between the opening of the banquet of sin and its close. Anyone looking in at its beginning might have said, "Oh the grandeur of Belshazzar's banquet!" But if you look in at its close, your blood curdles with horror. The King of Terrors, Death, has entered. Human blood is the wine, and dying groans are the music. Death always breaks in upon sin's banquet, sooner or later.

Every soul shall be weighed in the judgment scales of God. Is it possible you are weighed in God's balances, and are found wanting?

May we hear and heed God's message to our own hearts.

God's Banquet

There is another banquet to which we are all invited. It is described in Revelation 19:6-9. The invitation has an R.S.V.P. Have you made your reservation?

Gracious God, thank You for honoring me with Your royal invitation to the great banquet in heaven. By Your grace, I shall be there!

58

In the Lions' Den

Read Daniel 6

Daniel in the lions' den is one of the most familiar and beloved stories in the Bible.

The Prominence of Daniel

Now Daniel so distinguished himself among the administrators and the satraps by his exceptional qualities that the king planned to set him over the whole kingdom (6:3). Daniel was appointed to the number one position of seniority in the cabinet of King Darius. A veteran of some sixty years in public office, he now becomes the elder statesman of the empire of Babylon.

The Plot

A diabolical plot unfolds—*the administrators and the satraps tried to find grounds for charges against Daniel in his conduct of government affairs, but they were unable to do so. They could find no corruption in him, because he was trustworthy and neither corrupt nor negligent* (v. 4).

What a great tribute these words are to the integrity of Daniel. What exemplary and sterling qualities for any today who serve in high public office. These words should be emblazoned in the corridors of our places of government and public trust.

Those who monitored Daniel's public behavior to find some reportable offense had to acknowledge that Daniel was without fault: *We will never find any basis for charges against this man Daniel unless it has something to do with the law of his God* (v. 5).

In contrast to Daniel's sterling qualities, the other administrators resort to falsehood as they tell the king that *all agreed that the king should issue an edict.* They further resort to flattery as they request an edict that would require all the people to pray only to the king for the next thirty days. It is obvious why the plotters made prayer their main emphasis. They knew it was Daniel's habit to pray.

Any offender would be cast into the den of lions. An edict against prayer, a den of hungry lions, and a man whose devotion to his God is renowned—all make for a cunning plot indeed.

The Prayer Life of Daniel

The narrative reads: *Now when Daniel learned that the decree had been published, he went home to his upstairs room where the windows opened toward Jerusalem. Three times a day he got down on his knees and prayed, giving thanks to his God, just as he had done before* (v. 10).

Daniel sets for us an example of devotion and diligence in the spiritual life. We must ever keep the windows of our soul open to God, to let His light shine through, to allow Him to reveal Himself and His will to us.

The crises of our life simply reveal what we have been all along. They will uncover our strength or reveal our weakness. The person who faithfully follows the discipline of prayer and worship will be prepared and adequate for the testings of life.

We find Daniel giving thanks to God. Such is the paradox of the godly life. When circumstances are the most perilous, when danger and even death may await just outside the door, the believer can still give thanks.

GOOD LORD, I ASK NOT FOR AN EASY LIFE, BUT FOR ADEQUACY; NOT TO BE FREED FROM STORMS, BUT TO HAVE BUILT ON THE FOUNDATION OF A ROCK THAT WILL NOT FAIL.

59

God Is Able

Read Daniel 6

We have noted the prominence of Daniel, the plot that unfolds, and the prayer life of Daniel. The drama of Daniel in the lions' den now moves toward its climax and conclusion.

The Powerless King

Daniel prayed. The spies outside his window observed his activity of prayer. They had sprung their trap.

The conspirators quickly make their way to the king, and with contempt say that *Daniel, who is one of the exiles from Judah, pays no attention to you, O king, or to the decree you put in writing* (6:13). In other words, "That old Jew who is but a captive, and for whom you have done so much, has disregarded your decree and shows you disrespect."

The king now knows he has been tricked. He has been duped by their duplicity. The conspirators remind him that according to the laws of the Medes and Persians he cannot go back on his decree.

We read that the king was greatly distressed. He made every effort to rescue Daniel but in the end he was powerless. The order was given and Daniel was thrown into the lions' den. The trapped king resignedly says to Daniel, *May your God, whom you serve continually, rescue you!* (v. 16)

The den is sealed with a stone. The king spends a restless night. No doubt Daniel was able to sleep or rest better than the king, for there is no pillow as soft as a good conscience.

A Powerful God

The story moves on quickly: *At the first light of dawn the king got up and hurried to the lions' den. When he came near the den he called to Daniel in an anguished voice, Daniel . . . has your God, whom you serve continually, been able to rescue you from the lions?* (v. 20) Of course, God is able. Daniel answers that God had sent His angel, and *He shut the mouths of the lions* (v. 22). This great deliverance is immortalized in the heroes roll call of faith in Hebrews 11:33.

The Proclamation of the King

The king's sense of outrage is expressed by an immediate reversal of his edict and the summary punishment of the evil schemers who, "along with their wives and children," were thrown into the lions' den. They were immediately consumed by the wild beasts. We must remember that this is describing pagan laws of that time.

Daniel now enjoys further fame and prosperity. But his work is not done. He is yet to write his cyclorama of world events, the rise and fall of worldly empires, and the coming of the Ancient of Days to occupy the throne of the eternal kingdom.

Lord Jesus, teach me to pray. Take every faculty You have given and make it servant to the light You reveal.

60

THE FOUR BEASTS IN HISTORY

READ DANIEL 7

THE RIVER OF DANIEL 7 flows wide and deep. Empires rise and fall until the great consummation of the return of Christ. It provides a panorama of the grand course of history.

This chapter begins the second major division in Daniel. The first six chapters were primarily narrative, whereas the last six chapters are prophetical. In this second half of the book we have a series of Daniel's own visions.

Daniel relates nine times his personal experience, *I saw,* or *I beheld* (7:2, 4, 6-7, 9, 11, 13, 21). Chapter 7 is a record of the vision and revelation given to the great prophet.

THE FOUR BEASTS

Daniel is given a vision of four great beasts that come out of the sea. The first beast was as a lion with wings. This beast is an emblem of Babylon and symbolizes strength and swiftness. But then the wings were plucked from the beast, for Babylon's empire would be conquered by Persia.

The second beast that appears is as a bear. This represents the second in the succession of great empires—the Persian Empire. The bear was an apt symbol of the massive and ponderous military might of the Persian Empire. It has been suggested that the three ribs in his mouth represent the kingdoms of Babylon, Libya, and Egypt.

The third beast is as a leopard. This is symbolic of the Greek Empire which, under Alexander the Great, swiftly overcame its enemies. The amazing speed and striking power of Alexander which quickly laid Persia and the world at his feet is one of the great marvels of history. It has been suggested that the four heads of the leopard stand for the division of his empire after his death into the four kingdoms of Syria, Egypt, Macedonia, and Asia Minor.

The fourth beast is indescribable, its grotesque features defying classification, and its uncontrolled behavior brings great terror. This nondescript beast depicts the "Roman Empire." It is characterized by great power and fierce terror that *crushed and devoured its victims and trampled underfoot whatever was left* (7:7).

Daniel gives the interpretation: *The four great beasts are four kingdoms that will rise from the earth* (v. 17). The vision is prophetic of the four great world empires: Babylon, Medo-Persia, Greece, and Rome.

The "Ten Horns"

The fourth beast is described as having ten horns growing out of his head. They are most often interpreted as corresponding to a confederacy of ten kingdoms that will come out of the old Roman Empire. *The ten horns are ten kings who will come from this kingdom* (v. 24).

The "Little Horn"

Also springing out of the same head of the fourth wild beast and displacing three of the first horns was a "little horn." Many interpret this as symbolizing the antichrist, a human being with extraordinary intelligence and devastating power. In the interpretation given to Daniel, we learn that *he will speak against the Most High and oppress His saints and try to change the set times and the laws.* The saints will be handed over to him for a time, times and half a time (v. 25).

This is believed to represent the great persecution under the antichrist. However, his reign is short with the word "time" referring to one year, so that the total period of his reign will be three and one half years. This corresponds to the period of Daniel 12:7, the forty-two months of Revelation 11:2 and 13:5 and the 1,260 days of Revelation 11:3; 12:6. It is also the period of which our Lord spoke in His "Olivet Discourse" in Matthew 24:15.

But enough of this bad news. This chapter ends with good news—in fact, the grandest news of all history.

The story is told of a group of tourists in the Highlands of Scotland who saw a rare plant on the side of a cliff. There was no way to approach it. Upon seeing a boy helping his father keep the sheep in a field, they asked him to allow them to lower him over the cliff on a rope. The boy hesitated. They promised him a liberal reward. Finally he said he would do it under one condition. "I will do it," he said, "if my father holds the rope." We too can face with confidence the difficult and dangerous testings of life if we know we are in the hands of our Father.

As we continue with this chapter, we will see how history and the believer are in the mighty hand of God.

ETERNAL GOD, LET YOUR RIGHTEOUSNESS RULE OUR BELOVED COUNTRY IN EVERY PLACE OF COMMERCE AND JUSTICE AND IN EVERY HEART AND HOME.

61

The Grand Climax of History

Read Daniel 7:9-28

We have considered Daniel's vision and interpretation of the succession of the four great empires of history, and the terrible devastation of the end times with the coming of the antichrist. Daniel now ends with Good News—the grandest news of all history.

The Ancient of Days

The scene shifts from earth to heaven, from the terrestrial to the celestial, from the antichrist to Christ. The setting is similar to Revelation 4–5. The text breaks into poetic expression as Daniel exults:

> *Thrones were set in place, and the Ancient of Days took His seat. His clothing was as white as snow; the hair of His head was white like wool. . . . Thousands upon thousands attended Him; Ten thousand times ten thousand stood before Him. The court was seated, and the books were opened* (Dan. 7:9-10).

He who is called the "Ancient of Days" (vv. 9, 13, 22)

comes in the consummation of history. This great title, in reference to God the Father, speaks of His eternal existence. His pure white clothing and hair is emblematic of His purity and wisdom. The prophet's beatific vision is of Him clothed in ineffable light, and attended by multiplied millions.

He comes and takes away the dominion of the beast. He comes with judgment, and after destroying the power of the beast—*Then the sovereignty, power and greatness of the kingdoms under the whole heaven will be handed over to the saints, the people of the Most High. His kingdom will be an everlasting kingdom, and all rulers will worship and obey Him* (v. 27).

The saints, or God's people, will become joint-heirs with Christ (Rom. 8:15-17.) Someone has said, "Everybody must be somebody to somebody to be anybody." That is true of course on the human level. On the spiritual level, we are all children of the Heavenly King and heirs of the riches and glories of Christ's eternal kingdom. We are each somebody very special to God.

The Second Coming

This seventh chapter of Daniel is one of the greatest chapters in the Old Testament. Its prophecies have presented a panorama of history that culminates with the coming of the Messiah. Daniel in this chapter is given one of the greatest if not the grandest vision of all in the Old Testament.

> *In my vision at night I looked, and there before me was one like a son of man, coming with the clouds of heaven. He approached the Ancient of Days and was led into His presence. He was given authority, glory and sovereign power; all peoples, nations and men of every language worshiped Him. His dominion is an everlasting dominion that will not pass away, and His kingdom is one that will never be destroyed* (Dan. 7:13-14).

Daniel, centuries before Jesus was born, gives this dramatic and graphic prophecy of the glorious coming of Christ and His sovereignty over all peoples and His eternal kingdom.

Son of Man

This seventh chapter introduces one of the great titles of Christ—"Son of Man." It is a title Jesus used of Himself some eighty times in the Gospels. Its origin is in this messianic passage in Daniel. Thus Jesus' application of it identified Him with the messianic hopes of the people.

Jesus was intimately acquainted with the prophecies of His coming. When on trial before the Sanhedrin and put under oath by the high priest to tell who He really was, He answered, *you will see the Son of Man sitting at the right hand of the Mighty One and coming on the clouds of heaven* (Mark 14:62). Jesus was referring to this verse in Daniel 7:13 and everyone in that court knew it. The record states that then "the high priest tore his clothes . . . 'you have heard the blasphemy!' " It was that accusation that sent Him to the cross.

When Christ returns it will be a time of judgment—*The court was seated and the books were opened.* Only the blood of Christ has the power to expunge from the celestial archives the record of our sins and failures before God.

But on that day of judgment, for the believer, Christ will be our Advocate (1 John 2:1), and our Mediator (1 Tim. 2:5).

May we, with new meaning from this great passage, join in the song of praise by Robert Grant:

O worship the King, all glorious above;
O gratefully sing His power and His love;
Our shield and defender, the Ancient of Days,
Pavilioned in splendor and girded with praise.

Sovereign God, I hear and respond to the trumpet call of this text, that I may be found faithful at the mighty triumph of Your return.

62

DANIEL'S PRAYER

READ DANIEL 8:27–9:19

DANIEL WAS IN A STATE of exhaustion from the impact of the revelation he had received. But in the midst of his trauma we find he does three things.

First, he goes to his work—*Then I got up and went about the king's business* (8:27). Our Christian faith should make us more responsible in our daily tasks.

Second, Daniel searched the Scriptures. He makes specific reference to studying the writings of Jeremiah to gain understanding of the vision God had given to him. We too will find understanding for our perplexities and guidance for the future by our study and meditation on the Scriptures.

HIS PRACTICE OF PRAYER

Third, Daniel turned his care into prayer. William Law declared, "He who has learned to pray has learned the greatest secret of a holy and happy life." We observed in the story of Daniel being thrown into the lions' den that his fidelity in prayer was well known.

His Preparation for Prayer
Daniel did not approach God effortlessly. He came to God *in fasting and in sackcloth and ashes* (9:3).

Prayer is the highest art of the spiritual life. Like all arts, it has its disciplines. It is the most difficult exercise of the soul. It requires the most careful preparation of mind and heart and body. Too often we rush into prayer with preoccupied minds, tired bodies, unexamined lives, and self-centered requests.

But Daniel came in earnestness as evidenced by his fasting. He deprived his body that he might nourish his soul. He turned his thoughts from the physical to the spiritual. He came in sackcloth and ashes as a sign of his humility and penitence.

We would most carefully prepare ourselves for an audience with any great person. How much more should we most diligently and devotedly prepare ourselves to come into the presence of the Lord of the universe.

His Praise in Prayer
Daniel commences his prayer in a note of praise: *O Lord, the great and awesome God, who keeps His covenant of love with all who love Him and obey His commands* (v. 4).

We also need to come to God with a sense of awe and wonder at the greatness, the faithfulness, and the love of God.

His Penitence in Prayer
The dominant note of Daniel's prayer is penitence. He pray
we have sinned (v. 5). He identifies himself with thos
whom he was interceding. He goes down into the v
humiliation with his people. Although himself wit
his prayer is one of confession of sin and dee

Perhaps a Christian parent might be led t

weeks" as it is rendered in the *King James Version*. The NIV renders it "seventy sevens." The word *heptad* for "seven" is a unit measure. Bible scholars are almost unanimous that the seventy heptads or seventy weeks stand for seventy sevens of years, or 490 years.

God answered Daniel's prayer concerning Israel, the city of Jerusalem, and the sanctuary. But He also unveiled the entire panorama of history, from the end of the Babylonian Captivity to the end of time itself. He was given understanding that Israel's sojourn of seventy years in captivity was a type of a longer Dispersion, seven times as long.

This period of 490 years is "decreed" by God for the sixfold purpose which is given and subsequently identified as the work of the Messiah: *to finish transgression, to put an end to sin, to atone for wickedness, to bring in everlasting righteousness, to seal up vision and prophecy and to anoint the Most Holy* (v. 24). Here we have a comprehensive picture of the purpose and work of Christ—His triumph over sin and His everlasting kingdom.

The beginning of this timetable is given as: *From the issuing of the decree to restore and rebuild Jerusalem* (v. 25). It is essential that we have the right anchor date to understand this prophecy. There were three decrees starting with the one by Cyrus in 536 B.C. that allowed the Jews to return to Jerusalem. But these decrees do not encompass the details of this prophecy. But the second decree of Artaxerxes, issued in 445 B.C. (Neh. 2:4-8), involved the activity Gabriel described—*restore and rebuild Jerusalem . . . rebuilt with streets and a trench, but in times of trouble* (v. 25).

The timetable is all centered on the Messiah. All history centers on and has its fulfillment in Christ.

The "seventy sevens" are divided into three unequal segments. First there is the "seven sevens," or forty-nine years, which is the period from the decree to rebuild and restore

Jerusalem to the close of the Old Testament, or from 445 B.C. to 396 B.C.

The second segment is "sixty-two sevens" or 434 years, after which "the Messiah will be cut off." Here we have what many consider to be the most amazing prophecy in the Old Testament. Almost a half millennium in advance, the very year of the fulfillment of the ministry of Christ is predicted.

There are many theories over dates. A study of more than twenty writers showed varied timetables, but with one very significant consensus. All of their dates reckoned from Daniel's prophecy to the crucifixion of Christ fell within a nine year period, A.D. 27–36.

One of the most respected studies on these dates is that by Sir Robert Anderson of Britain. He notes that the year and day of Christ's death can be established with precision, due to Luke's reference that our Lord began His ministry "in the fifteenth year of Tiberius Caesar." Tiberius is known to have begun his reign on August 19, A.D. 14. Thus the fifteenth year of Tiberius' reign was A.D. 29. The Crucifixion took place at the fourth Passover of Jesus' ministry. The day that Jesus entered Jerusalem would have been Sunday, April 6, A.D. 32, exactly 173,880 days, which is equal to the 483 prophetic years of Daniel's vision. No wonder this is considered by many to be the most amazing prophecy of the Old Testament! Daniel prophesied to the very day, over four centuries in advance, "the cutting off of the Messiah."

The Messiah did come in the exact period prophesied. We have a "covenant-keeping" God. Jesus ratified upon Calvary God's covenant with man.

LORD OF HISTORY, WHOSE DESIGNS ARE INSCRUTABLE, HELP OUR NATION AND OUR GLOBAL VILLAGE TO KNOW THAT IN YOUR WILL ALONE IS OUR PEACE.

64

The Touch of God

Read Daniel 10

The Preparation

SPIRITUAL VISION IS DEPENDENT upon preparation and heart condition. It is the pure in heart who see God. Daniel tells us in this passage that he mourned and fasted for three weeks. Richard Foster in his excellent book, *Celebration of Discipline,* reminds us that fasting is one of the lost disciplines on the path to spiritual growth. There are some things that will come only by prayer and fasting.

The Presence

We find Daniel along the banks of the Tigris River, where he can more easily reflect and commune with God, away from official duties and the press of the world. Suddenly there is before him a glorious presence of transcendent beauty and ineffable radiance, robed like a priest. Many Bible commentators believe this was a theophany or preincarnate appearance of Christ to the Prophet Daniel. They call attention to the very close parallel of description with John's vision of Christ on Patmos (Rev. 1:13-16).

Daniel describes his being overwhelmed by such a glorious presence: *I had no strength left, my face turned deathly pale and I was helpless. . . . I fell into a deep sleep, my face to the ground* (Dan. 10:8-9). He further describes himself as trembling, speechless, and hardly able to breathe.

At the Transfiguration the three disciples fell facedown terrified and Jesus touched them and said, *Get up . . . don't be afraid* (Matt. 17:6-7). On Patmos John, before the glorified Christ, *fell at His feet as though dead,* and Jesus touched him and said, *Do not be afraid* (Rev. 1:17). Paul, on the Damascus Road, fell blinded before the dazzling radiance of Christ (Acts 9:3-9). It is an awesome experience to come into the presence of the Lord.

Daniel feels the touch of a hand upon him which sets him upon his feet. Four times in the Book of Daniel we find the statement: "He touched me" (8:18; 10:10, 16, 18). He knew the touch of the Almighty upon his life. That was the secret of Daniel's greatness.

We too can know the power and fresh vision that comes from the touch of God upon our lives. His touch will come to us when we most earnestly seek Him. Our constant prayer must be "Touch me again, Lord." We need His touch for each new task and circumstance.

Daniel now receives the answer and reassurance from his prayer. He is told, *Daniel, you are highly esteemed* (v. 11). He is further assured that since the first day of his praying, *your words were heard* (v. 12). True prayer is heard at once by God. We also see that prayer delayed is not prayer denied.

The Cosmic Powers

This "TV of Scripture" suddenly changes channels and flashes some of the most fascinating scenes ever "beamed" down to earth. The veil is drawn aside for us to see one of the most intriguing behind-the-scenes revelations of all time.

The divine messenger was delayed because *the prince of the Persian kingdom resisted me twenty-one days* (v. 13). John Walvoord suggests this is a fallen angel under the direction of Satan. There was a spiritual resistance to God's plan that required the intervention of the Archangel Michael, patron angel of the Jews.

There are unseen and cosmic forces that oppose the will of God. There is a great battle *against the spiritual forces of evil in the heavenly realms* (Eph. 6:12). There is an invisible conflict between the forces of good and evil. This earth is the battleground of war between the forces of good and evil. There are extraterrestrial forces in opposition to our prayers and God's will for us. We are utterly dependent on the power of prayer and God's help.

SOVEREIGN GOD, WITH THE ANONYMOUS POET I PRAY, "A REVELATION NEW OF WHAT THY GRACE CAN DO, O GOD, BE MINE! THE NEED IS ALL MY OWN, THE GRACE IS THINE ALONE, GRACE, DEEP AS NEED, MADE KNOWN, THY GRACE DIVINE."

65

HISTORY PREWRITTEN

READ DANIEL 11

AN OLD DEFINITION SAYS that "prophecy is history prewritten." This chapter contains the most detailed picture of future events found in the Old Testament. Its amazingly accurate description of history from before the time of Alexander the Great to the end time has led critics to claim a much later date for the Book of Daniel than that held by evangelical scholars.

C. Mervyn Maxwell gives an apt description of this passage: "It ranges over history, as if the angel who spoke it were a kind of cosmic Walter Cronkite reviewing headlines on TV and signing off, 'So that's the way it is'—or rather, since this is predictive prophecy, 'So that's the way it will be.' And like the evening headlines, almost every act reported in this chapter is a hostile one. Every actor appears in a bad light, fighting or preparing to fight someone."

This chapter has been the subject of many interpretations.

The "Football of the Nations"

Israel lay at the crossroads of the world. Whoever controlled that strategic area had a supreme military advantage. Its location as the bridge of the Middle East led it to become "the football of the nations." For its citizens, it was like living between the Hatfields and the McCoys! To its neighbors it became "that indigestible little country" that troubled both its suppressors and those it oppressed.

The prophecies in this chapter of the "kings of the south" and the "kings of the north" refer to their location relative to Palestine. To the west was the Mediterranean Sea and to the east was the Arabian Desert. Palestine became the battlefield for the wars of these kings and their empires. Its people would through the centuries be ground between these "upper and lower millstones."

The recorded history of man is marked by his succession of wars, rebellions, assassinations, and revolutions. Chapter 11 of Daniel is strewn with the litter of the warnings to and oppressions of the rebellious people. Gabriel's prophecy to Daniel takes us to broader and more distant scenes on his mural of prewritten history.

Antichrist to Armageddon

There has been general unity of opinion that verse 36 introduces the antichrist. He is the "man of lawlessness" Paul writes of in 2 Thessalonians 2:3-4. He is the "deceiver" that is coming as described by John (1 John 2:18, 22; 4:3; 2 John 7). He is the first "beast" of Revelation 13.

He will be successful until the time of wrath is completed, for what has been determined must take place (Dan. 11:36). The "time of wrath" is the great tribulation decreed by God to take place in the end time as recorded in Revelation 6–19.

Gabriel portrays the most profane and godless one: *The*

king will do as he pleases. He will exalt and magnify himself above every god and will say unheard-of things against the God of gods (Dan 11:36). Self-exaltation is a distinguishing feature and his blasphemous statements against God will be unparalleled.

We are into *the time of the end* (v. 40). Between verses 35-36 over 2,000 years have passed. Nothing in history has ever corresponded to verses 36-45. It is the final scene in the drama of history.

The antichrist plays one of the most strategic roles in the end time. He will be appealing to many and have incredible, persuasive power. He will be as an incarnate Satan. He will have control of the political and religious systems.

No man will be a match for the antichrist: *He will invade many countries and sweep through them like a flood. He will also invade the Beautiful Land* (vv. 40-41). Among the many countries to feel the onslaught of the antichrist will be Israel, which twice in this chapter is referred to as "the Beautiful Land." This land that was special to its people and their God would be desecrated by the violent warfare of the antichrist.

After prophesying the great conquests and dominion of the antichrist, the final word about him is: *Yet he will come to his end* (v. 45). The Apostle Paul tells us that the Lord Himself will vanquish him (2 Thes. 2:8).

The great battle of Armageddon is prophesied in Daniel 11:40-45. The antichrist *will set out in great rage to destroy and annihilate many* (v. 44). But he will meet his defeat in the War of Armageddon which will be by far the biggest, boldest, bloodiest, and most blasphemous of all wars. It will come at the end of the Tribulation.

God's special "war correspondent" of these last days, John, writes: *Then they gathered the kings together to the place that in Hebrew is called Armageddon* (Rev. 16:16).

Then I saw the beast and the kings of the earth and their armies gathered together to make war against the rider on the horse and his army. But the beast was captured, and with him the false prophet. . . . The two of them were thrown alive into the fiery lake of burning sulfur (Rev. 19:19-20).

The Things That Last

No age has known such ruthlessness and violence as ours. Daniel in his vision saw the transitory nature of man's power and the quick fading of his military might and glory.

When leaders of the world may be tempted to the same kind of madness which can take hold of men and nations, this book and its lessons can serve as a somber warning and beacon.

ETERNAL GOD, HELP US TO BE VIGILANT FOR THE CAUSE OF RIGHTEOUSNESS AND COURAGEOUS FOR THE CAUSE OF HOLINESS.

66

THE END!

READ DANIEL 12

THREE TIMES IN THE FIRST verse of chapter 12, we read, "At that time." It signals that this chapter relates to the final act of the drama of human history. Michael the archangel had just referred to "the time of the end" (11:40). We have been brought through the Tribulation, the period of antichrist and Armageddon.

Michael is introduced with full status. No longer is he simply "one of the chief princes" (10:13), or "your prince" (v. 21). But he is *Michael, the great prince who protects your people* (12:1). He is the patron angel and protector of Israel.

TROUBLE

There shall be a time of trouble, such as never was since there was a nation (v. 1, NKJV). Jesus echoed this ominous prophecy: *For then there will be great distress, unequaled from the beginning* (Matt. 24:21). The penman of Patmos terms this period *the Great Tribulation* (Rev. 7:14).

If "coming events cast their shadows before them" we are seeing some foreboding shadows on man's landscape. The threat of nuclear destruction is an ominous cloud over the horizon of every new generation. There are the dark shadows of overpopulation, wars, and civil strife, devastating famines, missiles with nuclear warheads poised around the world, international tensions, and environmental catastrophes. Are we not on the threshold of the perilous times prophesied by Daniel? Can we not foresee the word *Finis* on the canvas of history?

Triumph

But the great Book of Daniel does not end on the doleful note of trouble, but on the ringing note of triumph. It modulates from minor to major key in these final verses. It is like going from Tchaikovsky's *War of 1812* to his *Swan Lake*.

There will be deliverance. But it will be conditional deliverance—for *everyone whose name is found written in the book* (Dan. 12:1). Those whose names are in God's Book of Life will be saved.

Daniel gives a great prophecy: *Multitudes who sleep in the dust of the earth will awake: some to everlasting life, others to shame and everlasting contempt* (v. 2). Here in this verse the doctrine of resurrection breaks through into the faith of man as a sea beating at the dikes of human aspiration, which at last forces a breach and floods the human soul. The great truth dawns in this moment: God has made us for eternity.

With the prophecy of resurrection is one of the most radiant promises of the Bible: *Those who are wise will shine like the brightness of the heavens, and those who lead many to righteousness, like the stars for ever and ever* (v. 3). Is not Daniel his own best illustration of this truth? The mighty kings of his day have become merely a footnote on the pages of history compared to the radiant and enduring influence of Daniel.

Those who are wise in the things of God and those who are soul winners are God's stars. They reflect God's glory and bring His illumination to a darkened world.

Terminus

Daniel is told to *close up and seal the words of the scroll until the time of the end* (v. 4). The same book that is closed in Daniel 12 is opened in Revelation 10, when John the Seer describes the time of the end.

Loving God, make me a winner of souls and a star in Your kingdom.

67

Two Intriguing Prophecies

Read Daniel 12

Two hallmarks are given of the end time. First, "many shall run to and fro." Daniel never traveled faster than in a horse-drawn chariot. Today we have cars that can travel at 200 mph, rocket planes that hurtle through air at 4,000 mph, and spaceships that circle the earth at 18,000 mph. These astronomical accelerations have allowed an unprecedented increase in travel. Daniel's prophecy of speed and sky-rocketing mobility is happening in our day.

The second hallmark Daniel gives of the end time is that *knowledge shall increase.* We live in "the information age." The computer which burst upon the scene around 1950 with its mind-staggering capabilities has become a major force behind the knowledge explosion of our age. The silicon chip, "an educated grain of sand," has spawned astonishing knowledge, from the cells of the human body to the rings of Saturn. Today our orbiting telescopes probe the heavens and yield dramatic revelations about the universe. Daniel's prophecy of a knowledge explosion is a phenomenon of our day.

Alvin Toffler in his book *Future Shock* writes of the technological revolution of our day. He says that if the last 50,000 years of man's existence were divided into lifetimes of approximately 62 years each, there have been about 800 such lifetimes. And only within the present, the 800th lifetime, has the overwhelming majority of all the material goods we use in daily life been developed. Kenneth Boulding, eminent economist and imaginative social thinker, has stated: "The world of today . . . is as different from the world in which I was born as that world was from Julius Caesar's. . . . Almost as much has happened since I was born as happened before."

My generation has had its collision course with the future. Just think, I was before television, before radar, before split atoms, and before man walked on the moon. I was before air conditioners, frozen foods, dishwashers, credit cards, contact lenses, ballpoint pens, and before copy machines and faxes. McDonalds and instant coffee were unheard-of. So were tape decks and artificial hearts. Daniel's prophecy of increased knowledge is a hallmark of our day.

Daniel's prophecies of history and its climactic events dwarf the limited predictions of the futurists of our time. He obviously could not understand his prophecies, though today with the perspective of history and many prophecies being fulfilled, interpreters can understand them better than Daniel could.

This magnificent book of the Bible ends with Daniel confirmed as an heir to the resurrection, a ringing note of victory for the aged prophet: *You will rest, and then at the end of the days you will rise to receive your allotted inheritance* (12:13). Praise God, we too may share in that glorious promise!

LORD GOD, THANK YOU FOR THIS MAGNIFICENT BOOK OF DANIEL WITH ITS MARVELOUS REVELATIONS. I PRAISE YOU THAT BY YOUR GRACE I AM AN HEIR TO ITS PRECIOUS PROMISES.

Love Story

Love Story

Read Hosea 1–3

Hosea is the second greatest love story in the Bible, second only to the story of Christ. Hosea is the prophet of grace, the St. John of the Old Testament. The burden of his message is God's undying love and compassion for wayward Israel. This is the Gospel according to Hosea.

God speaks to Hosea and humankind through the personal tragedy of the prophet. His grief became a doorway of discovery for the world to see a portrayal of the grace of God. The deeper insights and lessons of life are often given in the crucible of suffering.

Hosea's story is not to be considered an allegory. It is straightforwardly narrated with no indication that it is to be understood as other than a true story.

Unfaithfulness

Hosea is shocked as he walks into his home. His three children are unattended. He calls for his wife Gomer, but there is no answer. He searches frantically through their small house but she is nowhere to be found.

He had been warned that this would occur. God had instructed him: *Go, take to yourself an adulterous wife* (1:2). She would become symbolic of God's message to Israel. In response, Hosea had married Gomer and three children were born of their marriage. God's judgment of Israel was revealed in the symbolic names given to the children, meaning: *Scattered, Not-Loved, Not-My-People.*

Israel, like Gomer, had been unfaithful and said, *I will go after my lovers* (2:5). They were bold and willful in their pursuit of sin.

But God, after their needed chastisement, in unfailing love, tenderly renews His covenant with them: *I will betroth you to Me forever* (v. 19).

REDEEMED

The love story is climaxed as God directs Hosea: *Go, show your love to your wife again, though she is loved by another and is an adulteress. Love her as the Lord loves the Israelites, though they turn to other gods* (3:1).

Hosea goes in search of his faithless wife who had abandoned her home, husband, and children for a life of shame. He finds her where she has sold herself in adultery, and from the slave market he buys her back. In loving discipline and restoration to chastity, he reconciles her to himself (vv. 2-3).

When Gomer abandoned her home and family and went after other lovers, Hosea could have given her a written notice of divorce and been done with her. Or, according to the law of the land, he could have had her stoned to death as an adulteress. He did not seek his legal rights but instead paid the price for her redemption and reconciliation.

We Are Gomer

It is the love story of each of our lives. We have been called to be the bride of Christ, His church, to be pure and faithful. But we have left Him in search of other loves. We have flirted with and gone after other gods. But God, the divine Lover of our souls, has searched to bring us back to Himself. He has paid the terrible price of our redemption on Calvary.

We are Gomer, on the auction block of sin. Satan bids for our soul. He bids pleasure, possessions, pride, prestige. But when all seemed lost, God sent Jesus Christ into the marketplace. He bid the price of His precious blood. There was no higher bid than that. He made the scarlet payment on Calvary for our eternal redemption.

Divine Lover of my soul, all my lasting joys are found in You alone. Keep me faithful and worthy of Your great love.

69

A Door of Hope

Read Hosea 2–5

YEARS AGO A SUBMARINE was rammed by another ship and quickly sank, trapping the entire crew in its prisonhouse of death. Rescue ships rushed to the scene of disaster off the coast of Massachusetts. The crew clung desperately to life as the oxygen slowly gave out.

A rescue diver placed his helmeted ear to the side of the vessel and listened. He heard a tapping noise. Someone was tapping out a question in the dots and dashes of the Morse Code. The question came slowly: "Is . . . there . . . any . . . hope?"

This is the cry of humanity: "Is there any hope?" Is there any hope for our torn and troubled world? But the fundamental question has to do with individual man. Is there hope for redemption from the enslavement and destruction of sin?

Centuries ago, Hosea had a marriage that many would have thought hopeless to rescue. Gomer, his wife, deserted him and their children and became a harlot, selling her body and soul to the cult of Baal. In the midst of his trauma and tragedy he heard God say that *He will make the Valley of Achor a door of hope* (2:15).

"Achor" meant "trouble." This valley of trouble was remembered for the sin of Achan that resulted in a disastrous defeat at Ai for the Israelites when Joshua was leading them through the Promised Land.

Humankind lives in a "valley of trouble." We are threatened with defeat and destruction. But a door of hope has opened to us. Usually we associate hope and strength with the mountaintops, in the rarefied air where wide horizons beckon and the spirit is elevated by the heights. But God promises to give hope in the valley, in the lowland where it is dark and dank. Hosea found it to be so in his otherwise hopeless tragedy, and his story becomes symbolic for all God's people.

This promise of hope was abundantly fulfilled by the One who came and announced, "I am the gate; whoever enters through Me will be saved" (John 10:9). Christ is our Door of hope. He is our entry into a life of promise, salvation, and eternal life.

God is, in the great phrase of Francis Thompson, "The Hound of Heaven." This Divine Pursuer seeks us out in our sin and rebellious condition. He woos and wins us by His love.

John Gowans has given eloquent expression to this love of God, in his lines from the musical, *Hosea:*

If human hearts are often tender,
And human minds can pity know,
If human love is touched with splendor,
And human hands compassion show.
Then how much more shall God our Father
In love forgive, in love forgive!
Then how much more shall God our Father
Our wants supply, and none deny!

LOVING GOD, THANK YOU FOR SEEKING US OUT IN OUR SIN AND LOST CONDITION, REDEEMING AND RECONCILING US TO YOURSELF.

70

"HALF-BAKED" CHRISTIANS

READ HOSEA 6–9

LOVE AS THE MORNING MIST

IN ONE OF THE MOST striking metaphors in the Bible, the fickle and fleeting devotion of Israel is described: *Your love is like the morning mist, like the early dew that disappears* (6:4). This text challenges our devotion to God to be constant. It needs to be more than an emotional expression that goes almost as quickly as it comes. We need a faith that, unlike the early morning mist and dew, will endure the blast of heat and the storms of the day.

HALF-BAKED CHRISTIANS

Hosea, the master of metaphor, says: *Ephraim is a flat cake not turned over* (7:8). He warns of the danger of being "half-baked." Modern examples are not hard to find. We have seen those who are so preoccupied with piety that they neglect the practical. Then we have known their opposites—activists who emphasize the practical and neglect the devotional. This one-sidedness is often the outcome of the things to which we give our time and energy.

We are a generation that can be informed but not enlightened. Our media may overwhelm us with facts from which we fail to derive meaning. "Half-baked Christian" is an oxymoron—a contradiction of terms. God calls us to a balanced life in Christ.

Reaping the Whirlwind

They sow the wind and reap the whirlwind (8:7) is the universal judgment for sin. There is a correspondence between what we choose to do and the results or consequences. The succeeding chapters of Hosea present a poignant profile of prostitute Israel's painful penalty for its faithlessness. Their history of anguish is summed up in the words: *Because they have not obeyed Him; they will be wanderers among the nations* (9:17). That prophecy has been pathetically fulfilled through the centuries.

The consequences of sin always outweigh the initial act and intention. As someone has said, "Deed is seed, which is multiplied in harvest." Israel had sown the seed of infidelity and reaped the harvest of destruction.

Many live by the code, "Sin now and pay later." God's Word reminds us, *The wages of sin is death, but the gift of God is eternal life in Christ Jesus our Lord* (Rom. 6:23). Praise God, for you have chosen life!

Lord, help me guard the thoughts, words, and deeds that I sow each day, knowing that they reap character and destiny.

71

"A CALL FROM HOME"

READ HOSEA 10–14

THE ELEVENTH CHAPTER of Hosea is the love chapter of the book. It is the John 3:16 of the Old Testament. In one of the most tender and heart-warming passages of the Bible we are given a portrait of God's unquenchable love for sinful man.

God speaks through His prophet: *When Israel was a child, I loved him, and out of Egypt I called My son. . . . It was I who taught Ephraim to walk, taking them by the arms . . . it was I who healed them. I led them with cords of human kindness, with ties of love; I lifted the yoke from their neck and bent down to feed them* (11:1-4). This passage evokes the tender scene of a father holding his son by the hands as he takes his first faltering steps; of an anxious parent keeping watch by the bedside of a sick child; of feeding the child too young to feed itself. This portrait of God caring for us as a father for his child is unmatched in the Old Testament.

It is God's love story for humankind. He called each

of us "out of Egypt." Egypt is not merely a location, it is a condition. He called us from a life of bondage to a life of liberty. When we were helpless, He took us by the hand and taught us how to walk in His ways. He has healed our spiritual blindness and our hurts. When we needed to be nourished, He fed us with His word and truth. What divine condescension! What unfathomable love!

Return, O Israel, to the Lord your God (14:1) is the closing message of this great book. No less than fifteen times we hear God shouting through the Prophet Hosea, "Return."

Someone once asked Dwight L. Moody to define repentance. He said the best definition he ever heard was given by a soldier who, when asked how he was converted, answered: "The Lord said to me, 'Halt! Attention! Right-about-face! March!' "

The "right-about-face," the turning in the opposite direction, is the most difficult part. Man finds it hard to repent because he does not want to leave those things to which he has become attached.

Hosea is quoted over thirty times in the New Testament, more than any other of the minor prophets. His love story is our love story. Gomer, though unfaithful and fallen, was restored. So may we be by the grace of Christ. God says to all who will repent and return to Him: *I will heal their waywardness and love them freely, for My anger has turned away from them* (14:4).

May our response to the magnificent message of this book be as in its epilogue: *Who is wise? He will realize these things. Who is discerning? He will understand them* (14:9).

"LOVE DIVINE, ALL LOVES EXCELLING," WHO AS A FATHER HAS TENDERLY LOVED AND CARED FOR US, HELP ME TO EVER BE YOUR FAITHFUL AND LOVING CHILD.

FROM GLOOM TO GLORY

72

DAY OF THE LOCUSTS

READ JOEL 1:1–2:27

THE BOOK OF JOEL was prompted by national panic during an unparalleled plague of locusts. Joel sees the plague as a solemn warning of the judgment of God to come. His response to this unmitigated calamity is a call to repentance for the day of reckoning.

The Day of the Lord, Joel's great phrase, occurs five times (1:15; 2:1, 11, 31; 3:14) and is the dominant theme of his book. It can refer to the intervention of God in history as well as the coming of Christ in the consummation of the ages.

The desolation through the land is expressed with staccato poetry and stirring imagery appropriate for the overtones of war (2:3-11). The prophet gives one of the most eloquent passages on divine compassion: *Rend your heart and not your garments. Return to the Lord your God, for He is gracious and compassionate, slow to anger and abounding in love* (v. 13).

It is not the outward ritual but the inward contrition and change of heart that marks true repentance. It has been said that true repentance looks upon things past with a weeping eye and upon the future with a watchful eye. Repentance radically changes a person's behavior.

A granddaughter of Aaron Burr gave her heart to Christ in an evangelistic meeting. That evening she said to her grandfather, "I wish you were a Christian too." He replied, "When I was a young man I too went to an evangelistic meeting and felt my need of God's forgiveness. But I walked out without doing it and looking up toward heaven said, 'God, if You don't bother me anymore, I'll never bother You.' Honey, God has kept His part of the bargain and now it is too late for me to bother Him." A life of dishonor followed his fateful decision and unrepentance.

The message of Joel becomes a parable of human life. The locusts of sin have stripped away that which is green and wholesome and have devastated the life. Sin afflicts the life with spiritual drought, languishing in barrenness.

A return to God and repentance brings restoration, and ultimately the Holy Spirit and fruitfulness for the kingdom. All of this takes place because of a compassionate God and an obedient heart.

God, whose love is mediated through sunsets and rain, and through the truths of Your Word, help me to ever have an obedient heart and a ready hand to do Your will.

73

THE PROMISE OF THE HOLY SPIRIT

READ JOEL 2:1–3:21

THE PROMISE OF THE HOLY SPIRIT is the high-water mark of the Book of Joel. God declares: *I will pour out My Spirit on all people. Your sons and daughters will prophesy, your old men will dream dreams, your young men will see visions. Even on My servants, both men and women, I will pour out My Spirit in those days* (2:28-29).

This promise became the text for Peter's sermon on the Day of Pentecost (Acts 2:16-21). When others saw the startling results of Pentecost they thought the disciples were intoxicated. Peter defended their experience by interpreting the event as the fulfillment of Joel's prophecy: "This is what was spoken by the Prophet Joel."

The peerless promise of the Holy Spirit is for all believers. The bestowal of God's most precious gift is universal. It breaks down barriers of age, sex, and class—it is for the young and old, for men and women; there is no distinction between servants and free. All are equal before God and in His providence.

Salvation for All

And everyone who calls on the name of the Lord will be saved (Joel 2:32) is the evangelistic proclamation of the prophet. This text too was quoted verbatim by Peter on the Day of Pentecost and the result was 3,000 converts.

God's grace and gift of salvation is available to all. No one is outside of His love and mercy. Because Christ died for all, anyone can call on His name and be saved.

Sarah Graham wrote a hymn in the last century that speaks of God's grace for us on Calvary:

On the cross of Calvary,
Jesus died for you and me;
There He shed His precious blood,
That from sin we might be free.
O the cleansing stream does flow,
And it washes white as snow!
It was for me that Jesus died
On the cross of Calvary.

O what wondrous, wondrous love
Brought me down at Jesus' feet!
O such wondrous, dying love
Asks a sacrifice complete!
Here I give myself to Thee,
Soul and body, Thine to be;
It was for me Thy blood was shed
On the cross of Calvary.

Valley of Decision

Multitudes, multitudes in the valley of decision! (3:14) cries out the prophet. We are reminded that each person must make a choice concerning Jesus Christ. Pilate's words, "What shall I do with Jesus?" is the inescapable and pivotal question of every life. The answer determines our eternal destiny.

In the Olivet Discourse of our Lord just before His arrest and crucifixion, He borrowed the language of Joel to describe the judgment day to come when *the sun and moon will be darkened, and the stars no longer shine* (v. 15).

But the final word of the prophet is the promise of blessings for God's people (vv. 17-21). God's people will be blessed with security, peace, fruitfulness, and the Lord's presence. *The Lord dwells in Zion!* is the grand climax of Joel's prophecy.

The prophet has taken us from the swarming locusts to the peace of Zion, from calamity to calm, from gloom to glory. And so it is with everyone who puts their trust in God.

Heavenly Father, I praise You for Your limitless power, Your unsearchable wisdom and infinite love. Teach me how to trust You for time and eternity.

A Message for the Ages

74

God's Nobodies

Read Amos 1

One of the shepherds of Tekoa is the way Amos introduces himself in the book that has become one of the most relevant and powerful portions of the Word of God. His was a simple life, working in the outdoors, close to God's handiwork in nature.

Amos was not a professional preacher but a common farmer who knew God and was anointed by Him. He speaks intimately of God no less than eighty times in his nine chapters. Later in his book he amplifies his calling: *I was neither a prophet nor a prophet's son, but I was a shepherd, and I also took care of sycamore-fig trees. But the Lord took me from tending the flock and said to me, "Go, prophesy to My people Israel"* (7:14-15).

In the School of Obscurity

God seems to prepare His servants in secret for the work He later calls them to do in public. There was Moses in the backside of the desert; Gideon on the threshing floor; David on the hillside with his sheep; John the Baptist in the desert; Peter in his fishing boat; Paul in Arabia; Amos following the flock in the wilderness of Tekoa.

Only the one who has learned of God in the school of obscurity is entrusted to speak for Him among the crowds. As Amos was tending his sheep and fruit trees, God was preparing and fashioning him to become a mighty prophet with a message that would speak to the ages.

God's Nobodies

Amos also illustrates for us how God uses the insignificant to accomplish His purpose. Moses, the great lawgiver and one of the greatest leaders of all time, was born of slaves and of a nation downtrodden for four centuries. Yet God took this nobody and through him brought about the Exodus and gave the law of the Old Testament.

David was the youngest in his family and no one thought him to be important. Even Samuel, when he went to the house of Jesse to anoint the next king, was shown Jesse's other seven sons, no one thinking that the chosen one could be David who was out in the field "tending the sheep." From the most humble beginning God raised up Israel's greatest king.

It was not from the fabled cities of Athens or Rome, but from obscure Bethlehem that God brought forth the marvel of the ages.

The disciples of our Lord were all chosen from obscure backgrounds. None of them had any special credentials. But from their common clay of humanity were fashioned men who turned the world upside down.

And God has been doing the same through the centuries. St. Francis says that when God called him He took the meanest and smallest person He could find. God does His mighty works through Martin Luther, an obscure monk; William Booth, an itinerant evangelist among the outcast of London who founded The Salvation Army; Fanny Crosby, a blind poet who was inspired to write over 6,000 hymns; Corrie ten Boom, a simple Dutch woman who gave our century one of its most shining examples of love that sacrifices all for Christ; Joni, a quadriplegic who leads a world ministry in our day. Amos was but one of a succession of God's servants brought from obscurity to a mighty ministry.

Perhaps it is so that the glory may go to the Lord and not to mere mortals. Paul reminds us of this truth: *Brothers, think of what you were when you were called. Not many of you were wise by human standards; not many were influential; not many were of noble birth. But God chose the foolish things of the world to shame the wise; God chose the weak things of the world to shame the strong. He chose the lowly things . . . and the things that are not—to nullify the things that are, so that no one may boast before Him* (1 Cor. 1:26-29).

The Lion Roars

The tenor of the opening words of Amos flings out the burden and theme of his message: *The Lord roars from Zion and thunders from Jerusalem* (Amos 1:2). His is a message of judgment of God for the heinous sins and rebellion of Israel and Judah, a proclamation of approaching doom.

The herdsman from Tekoa has a message we need to hear today. Stay tuned!

Lord, thank You for taking the small offering of my life and blessing and using it for Your glory.

75

When Preaching Becomes Meddlin'

Read Amos 2

Amos is the first of the literary prophets, the earliest of those whose utterances have been recorded in books that bear their names. His writing inaugurated the great succession that has come down to us from the crises of their day.

Though a simple herdsman and not schooled in the guild of the prophets, he skillfully employs his homely epigrams and metaphors. One scholar says of Amos that he writes "with the poetic skill of a Euripides, and the naked prose of an Ernest Hemingway." Amos speaks with a forceful eloquence that resonates through the centuries with a relevant message for us today.

Popular Preaching

Amos, the roughly clad peasant turned prophet, had never studied the psychology of preaching, but he displays a rare forensic skill in the order and content of his message. His eloquence captures a growing audience.

To the delight of his auditors he starts out talking about his neighbors' sins. He begins with a condemnation of the "sins of Damascus" and proceeds to give God's indictment against six of the traditional enemies of Israel. No doubt his listeners are smugly pleased as he denounces their foes and their trafficking in human beings, their cruel slaughter of the defenseless, their desecration and pagan ways.

Perhaps some would have shouted the equivalent of "That's preaching!" "Amen, brother!" "That's telling it like it is!" as their enemies were pronounced guilty of violent behavior in human relations.

Meddlin' Message

Amos has been skillfully moving closer with each oracle. Now he turns to Judah, the Southern Kingdom. Although the enthusiasm of his hearers may have diminished, they were perhaps tolerant as he then spoke his oracle against Judah. But now his message takes a dramatic turn. He no longer is preaching against sins of human relationship but of man against God. *They have rejected the law of the Lord* (Amos 2:4) is their indictment.

At last his net is drawn and all of a sudden, reminiscent of Nathan's confrontation of David's sin (2 Sam. 12:7), Amos declares Israel to be the object of God's judgment and doom. With Israel he does not stop with one sin as he has done with the others but goes on to cite seven transgressions against God. They are guilty of economic and judicial injustice and of forsaking God. At this point we can almost hear his listeners saying, "This man has stopped preaching and now he's meddlin'."

It's all well and good when the preacher is taking others to task for their sins, but let's not get personal. It's OK to talk about the sins of Iran and other nations, but let's not condemn our own lifestyle and country. Let's not assault our national self-righteousness or our religious traditions.

Amos charges, *They sell the righteous for silver, and the needy for a pair of sandals. They trample on the heads of the poor as upon the dust of the ground and deny justice to the oppressed* (Amos 2:6-7). Added to their sin of economic oppression and injustice is the sin of immorality: *Father and son use the same girl and so profane My holy name* (v. 7).

Timely Thunder

The message of Amos, tragically, is not all that remote from our time and place. Do we know nothing of the exploitation of the poor, the lack of justice for the needy, a gross immorality that pervades the nation, a forsaking of the God of our fathers?

Let the thunder of Amos reverberate once more among us. Let us hear the prophetic Word of God, speaking not about the sins of others, but our own need of repentance and forgiveness. Let us beware lest our prosperity turn to ruin and our security to doom. God will not always tolerate our rebellion and sin. There comes a day of judgment as surely in our time as in that of Amos.

God, Judge of the universe, help me to see my own sin in the light of Your Word, to repent and do Your will.

76

To Whom Much Is Given

Read Amos 3

LIFE WILL BE JUDGED by its endowments. Jesus said, "For everyone to whom much is given, from him much will be required" (Luke 12:48, KJV).

Israel had the greatest endowment of all the nations of the earth. *You only have I chosen of all the families of the earth* (Amos 3:2) is the word of the Lord through the prophet to Israel. They were His chosen nation—not by any merit of their own but by His sovereignty and grace. God had brought them out of Egypt (2:10; 3:1), had given them the prophets (2:11), had favored them with His promises and providence. But they had turned against His love and commandments. God says to them, *Therefore I will punish you for all your sins* (3:2).

Walking with God

Amos now plies them with seven rhetorical questions to emphasize the impending judgment of God. Astute preacher and writer that he is, there is a progression from the lesser to the greater. The first is: *Do two walk together unless they have agreed?* (3:3) Concord is the requisite of companionship. Walking together implies a harmonious relationship. To walk with God requires that we be in agreement with His Word and will.

It is life's greatest privilege to know and walk with God. But with that supreme privilege comes a sacred responsibility.

THE LION HAS ROARED

Many oft-repeated words in this book betray the tenor of the content. Portentous words frequently occur such as: evil, punishment, transgression, trumpet, famine, calamity, tumult, wailing, woe, darkness, needy, remnant, oppress, devour, mourn, perish, and slay. He targets his message of doom to those of extravagant indulgence at the expense of the poor.

Then, speaking from his shepherd's experience, he says their destruction will be as that when sheep are attacked by a lion and all the shepherd can find may be "two leg bones . . . a piece of an ear" (v. 12). All their luxuries will be taken away: *I will tear down the winter house along with the summer house; the houses adorned with ivory will be destroyed and the mansions will be demolished, declares the Lord* (v. 15).

Our text reminds us of the truth in the couplet: "Only one life, will soon be past; Only what's done for Christ will last." All life's trinkets and treasures will fade away or be taken from us. But life eternal is the gift of Christ to His followers.

DAY OF ACCOUNTABILITY

Israel is cited as being zealous in their worship and faithful in their tithes (4:4-5). But their hearts were far from God. Today it still happens that we can observe the forms of religion but miss its substance. Legalism can replace true holiness and devotion. The mechanics can substitute for the dynamics of our faith.

God of the prophets, help me day by day, moment by moment, to live in Your presence and to do Your will.

77

A Firebrand Plucked from the Burning

Read Amos 4:1-11

He was a boy of five on the winter night when his family's house was swept away in flames. A nurse carried his five-month-old brother, Charles, to safety. But he was by an upstairs window surrounded by flames. Many onlookers felt that there was no way he could be rescued and his father, thinking him lost, commended his soul to God. But a man stood beneath the window and another climbed upon his shoulders and was able to take the boy in his arms and lower him to safety. At that very moment the roof fell in and the flames consumed the spot where he had been standing only seconds before.

The boy never forgot that event. Throughout his life that boy, John Wesley, referred to himself as "a brand snatched out of the burning."

Amos says to the people of Israel: *And you were like a firebrand plucked from the burning* (4:11, NKJV), or as the NIV renders it, *you were like a burning stick snatched from the fire.* Israel indeed was a firebrand plucked out of the burning. And so are we. Each of us was on the brink of destruction and are saved by the grace of God. Christ, at the tremendous cost of His own life, came to us in the midst of the fire of sin, stretched out His loving arms to us, and plucked us from destruction.

T. DeWitt Talmage, a preacher of yesteryear (1832–1902), tells the story of a soldier who, worn out in his country's service, took to the violin as a mode of earning his living. He was found in the streets of Vienna, playing his violin. But after a while his hand became feeble and tremulous, and he could no longer make music. One day, while he sat there despondent, a man passed his way and said, "My friend, you are too old and feeble; give me your violin."

He took the man's violin and began to discourse the most exquisite music. The people gathered around in larger and larger numbers, and the aged man held his hat, and the coins poured in until the hat was full.

"Now," said the man who was playing the violin, "put that coin in your pockets." The coin was put in the old man's pockets. Then he held his hat again and the violin played more sweetly than ever, and played until some of the people wept, and some shouted. Again the hat was filled with coin.

Then the violinist dropped the instrument and passed off, and the whisper went up, "Who is it?" Someone just entering the crowd said, "Why, that is Bucher, the great violinist, known through all the realm."

The fact was, he had just taken that man's place, and assumed his poverty, and bore his burden and played his music, and earned his livelihood, and made sacrifice for the poor old man. So the Lord Jesus comes. He finds us in our spiritual penury, and across the broken strings of His own broken heart He strikes a strain of infinite music which wins the attention of earth and heaven. He takes our poverty. He plays our music. He weeps our tears. He dies our death.

All this Christ did for you and me that He might pluck us from the burning.

DEAR SAVIOR, THANK YOU FOR REACHING OUT AND SAVING ME FROM SIN AND ITS ETERNAL DESTRUCTION.

78

Prepare to Meet Your God

Read Amos 4:12-13

The thunderclap of Amos' message is now sounded: *Prepare to meet your God* (4:12). The moment of ultimate accountability for Israel has come. An awesome encounter with the offended Jehovah cannot be avoided.

Meeting God on the Day of Judgment is the one inevitability of history for each of us. Sooner or later we must each meet our God. But the judgment of God need not be retributive. For those who have been faithful in love and obedience to Him, it will be remunerative. God has joy and rewards that transcend anything we have known on earth. May we indeed be prepared to meet our God.

An old song, written by "Anon," still speaks its solemn message:

Your garments must be white as snow, Prepare to meet your God:
For to His throne you'll have to go; Prepare to meet your God.

People make elaborate preparations for meeting an important person. They will pay great attention to their appearance, preparation of thought, precision of schedule, observance of protocol, etc. But some never think of their preparation to meet the Creator of the universe and the Savior of the world. May you and I, dear reader, be prepared to meet our God. If we are not prepared at this moment, let us put aside everything else and make this the top priority of our lives.

God's Terrible Repudiation

Israel's stubborn rebellion against God is to receive His final judgment. He denounces their oppression: *You trample on the poor* (5:11). He rebukes them for injustice, extortion, political and social evils.

Some of the auditors of Amos may have felt smug for their religious observances. They faithfully kept the religious feasts and brought offerings. But the herdsman of Tekoa now from his quiver draws his sharpest arrow to pierce their shallow religiosity with God's terrible repudiation: *I hate, I despise your religious feasts; I cannot stand your assemblies. . . . Away with the noise of your songs! I will not listen to the music of your harps* (vv. 21-23).

In one of the grand passages of the Bible, Amos thunders: *But let justice roll on like a river, righteousness like a never-failing stream* (v. 24). God does not want religious rites. He wants right relationships with Himself and others. God does not want the letter of the law but rather the spirit of the law as expressed in justice, love, and compassion. God does not want outward forms but rather a religion of the heart.

May we be prepared to meet our God. Then we too shall be a "firebrand plucked from the burning."

Help me, my God, to make the top priority of my life to be prepared for that inevitable day when I shall stand before Your judgment throne.

79

At Ease in Zion

Read Amos 6–9

WOE TO YOU WHO ARE at ease in Zion (6:1, NKJV) is God's warning to Israel. They were complacent because of their outward religious observances. Also, they trusted in the security that they thought would come from the military advantages of Samaria to the north. But God reminds them that greater nations than they have come to ruin, that their luxuries are doomed, and that they will be carried into exile (6:2-14).

Complacency still plagues the church and God's people. It remains one of the deadly sins. Let us beware that our security not be in outward forms, in religious organization or rites, but in a vital relationship with Jesus Christ.

Measured with a Plumb Line

Amos is granted a vision of Israel's impending doom (7:1-6). Then he shares the solemn warning from a vision of common imagery to the people of his day: *The Lord was stand-*

ing by a wall that had been built true to plumb, with a plumb line in His hand (v. 7). A plumb line is string with a weight on the end of it. It measures any deviation from a true vertical with the weight being pulled down by gravity while held by the string.

The vision is of the Lord taking measure of the uprightness of Israel. Israel "had been built true to plumb." God had chosen her and had established upright standards. As a wall that is leaning and tottering, Israel does not pass God's test and must be brought down.

Now the Good News!

The final word from Amos is one of Israel's restoration: *In that day I will restore David's fallen tent. I will repair its broken places, restore its ruins, and build it as it used to be* (9:11). God promises: *I will bring back My exiled people Israel; they will rebuild the ruined cities and live in them. . . . I will plant Israel in their own land, never again to be uprooted from the land I have given them, says the Lord your God* (vv. 14-15).

We have seen the beginning of that miracle take place since May 14, 1948 when Israel was restored as a nation after centuries of worldwide dispersion. How marvelous are the promises and providence of God.

It is believed that "the tabernacle of David" (9:11, NKJV) is in reference to the Messiah. How beautiful is the righteousness and compassion of God that such a radiant messianic promise comes from the prophet who spent most of his time predicting the downfall and doom of sinful people. Even out of prophetic gloom comes prophetic glory.

The humble herdsman from Tekoa was used of God to proclaim a message that was to have its fulfillment in the headlines of our day. Surely God's message through Amos is timely and timeless.

May it speak to our hearts and needs and may we heed what the Lord has to say to us through His prophet.

SAVE ME, GOOD LORD, FROM THE SIN OF COMPLACENCY. HELP ME TO REMEMBER THAT SATAN HAS NO CEASE-FIRES IN HIS BATTLE FOR OUR SOULS.

National Insecurity

80

National Insecurity

Read Obadiah

Obadiah is the shortest book in the Old Testament and the only book with just one chapter. But it packs a powerful message.

There are about a dozen men named Obadiah in the Old Testament, the name meaning "servant of the Lord." But the author is unique among the prophets in that he exclusively directs his message to the nation of Edom.

The Edomites literally lived *in the clefts of the rock* (v. 3). They considered their position impregnable. For generations they had dwelt secure in their impenetrable strongholds high up in the rocky gorges. Petra, their capital, along with their chief cities, had been carved out of the rock.

Obadiah punctures their inflated pride of security with the Lord's prophecy of their doom:

> *"The pride of your heart has deceived you, you who live in the clefts of the rocks and make your home on the heights, you who say to yourself, 'Who can bring me down to the ground?' Though you soar like the eagle and make your nest among the stars, from there I will bring you down," declares the Lord* (vv. 3-4).

In poetic hyperbole, the prophet describes their high position as "among the stars." And though they lived like the eagle, safely secluded in their high aeries, they will be brought down.

Within four years after the burning of Jerusalem, Edom was raided and left desolate by the Babylonians (vv. 11-15). With the destruction of Jerusalem in A.D. 70, the Edomites disappeared from history, fulfilling this awesome prophecy.

Do we not know something of a pride in national security? Of a sense of impregnability? Of a nation that has soared to great heights like the eagle and known to be among the stars? Do not the message and metaphors of the prophet have application to our nation?

And do we not know something of the enemies that lurk from within? The deceptions and the dangers that infiltrate and threaten to destroy? Of a national security based on its position and prowess?

No doubt the nuclear age, with its ominous threat of instant apocalypse, has awakened us to the fragility of our security. Our generation has been stirred to a sense of vulnerability as never before in the history of our nation. Our national security is no longer taken for granted. It is considered by many to be gravely imperiled.

The message of Obadiah should remind us that there is no such thing as national security. The most impregnable defenses always prove to be insecure in the end. History is replete with dramatic examples chronicled in the wars and conquests of man.

This Old Testament book is a wake-up call to us today that God alone is the security of the believer and the nation.

GOD OF HISTORY, LEST WE FORGET, KEEP OUR NATION MINDFUL OF YOUR SOVEREIGNTY AND GRACE.

God of the Second Chance

81

Running from God

Read Jonah 1:1-3

It is midnight on the Mediterranean and the sea rages in savage fury. The pagans, gathered around the light of the swinging lantern on the deck of their tempest-tossed ship, call on whatever gods they know to deliver them. Anxiety reflects on each face as lots are cast to see *who is responsible for this calamity* (1:7). These seasoned sailors had never seen a storm as violent as this. And the record reads, *the lot fell on Jonah* (v. 7).

The mariners then ask Jonah, *Tell us, who is responsible for making all this trouble for us? What do you do?* (v. 8) That question jolts him to realize who he is and he answers, *I am a Hebrew and I worship the Lord, the God of heaven, who made the sea* [that was the God they needed just then] *and the land* [where they wanted most to be] (v. 9).

Jonah's answer terrified them for they knew they were in the hands of an angry God. We read, *The sea was getting rougher and rougher. So they asked him, "What should we do to you to make the sea calm down for us?"* (v. 11)

Pick me up and throw me into the sea, he replied, and it will become calm (v. 12). After further vain efforts of rowing, *when the sea grew even wilder than before,* they reluctantly took *Jonah and threw him overboard, and the raging sea grew calm.* The mariners, awed at the sudden calm, then and there turned to Jehovah.

The Downward Course

The word of the Lord had come to Jonah to go and preach to Nineveh, but Jonah ran away from the Lord. He went down to Joppa. The path of disobedience to God is always downward. It was down to Joppa, down to the hold of the ship, down to the belly of the fish, down to the depths of the sea. The path away from God is a slippery slope that leads down, down, down to defeat and a maelstrom of destruction, unless we allow God to turn us back to Himself.

The sea may look calm and inviting at first, and the boat appealing, but the way from God always leads to a tempest.

Paying the Fare

The account tells us that Jonah "paid the fare." We always pay the fare when we try to run away from God. We pay the fare in inner conflict, guilt, and defeat. Sin is its own punishment and if we cannot live with God we find we cannot live at peace with ourselves.

Jonah never did get to his intended destination, nor did he get a refund on his ticket. Disobedience always exacts a high fare and gives nothing but trouble in return.

Running from God

Like many of us, Jonah struggled with obedience to God's word and will. A convenient alternative to God's will can often be found close by. Jonah found a ship going to Tarshish.

Nineveh was east, Tarshish was west. Jonah wanted to get as far away as possible from where God wanted him to go.

"Why did Jonah head the opposite way?" Nineveh was the capital of the mighty Assyrian Empire. It was surrounded by a wall 100 feet thick and wide enough for three chariots to drive abreast upon it. Its walls had 1,500 towers which were 100 feet high. Lions and bulls carved out of stone guarded its gates. For an alien prophet to come alone into such a city on behalf of an unknown God and pronounce doom upon it for its wickedness was indeed a dangerous and seemingly ludicrous mission. Surely it was an intimidating assignment.

But further into the narrative we learn the true reason for Jonah's disobedience. He admits he knew the Lord was gracious and he feared the constant and dreaded enemy of Israel might repent and be spared (4:1-2). It would be as if God told a Jew during World War II to go to Nazi Germany and preach repentance or doom. Simon Peter had a similar assignment (Acts 10) and needed God's prodding and providence to bring the Gospel to the Gentiles.

There is still the danger of wanting to share the Gospel only with those with whom we are familiar and comfortable. Our prejudices and bigotry can keep us from going where people need our caring and compassion most. The story of Jonah is a compelling statement on the universality of a Gospel that knows no barrier of nationality or race.

Jonah should have known he could not run away from God. The psalmist reminds us in his immortal words that there is no place we can flee from His presence (Ps. 139:7-10). There is no escape from God. Anyone who tries to run away from God is headed for a storm.

DIVINE GUIDE, SAVE ME FROM GOING MY OWN WAY AND HEADING IN THE WRONG DIRECTION WHEN YOU HAVE A TASK FOR ME TO DO.

82

The Great Fish

Read Jonah 1:4–2:10

THEN THE LORD SENT *a great wind on the sea, and such a violent storm arose that the ship threatened to break up* (1:4). The sailors followed the nautical practice of throwing cargo overboard to lighten the ship but the sea only got rougher. As we have seen, the situation called for Jonah to be thrown overboard. Then the record states, *But the Lord provided a great fish to swallow Jonah, and Jonah was inside the fish three days and three nights* (v. 17).

Many have refused to "swallow the whale" of Jonah's story. There are those who sneer at "Jonah's whale" that could swallow a man. They say the anatomical structure of a whale makes it impossible. Actually the Bible does not say "whale"; the accurate translation is "a great fish." But it does not matter either way.

The sperm whale, which in early ages frequented the Mediterranean, has a mouth twenty feet long, fifteen feet high, and nine feet wide, quite adequate for swallowing a person. Whalers have found giant squid larger than a man in the stomachs of sperm whales.

The *Princeton Theological Review* in 1927 reported on this subject: "Physiological tests entirely disprove the alleged impossibility of the story [of Jonah]. It is shown by study of the structure of the sperm whale and its habits that it is perfectly possible for a man to be swallowed alive and after an interval vomited up again, also for him to remain alive for two or three days within the whale. Historical tests show that a similar event has happened in later times in at least one case."

The article reports of a sailor, James Bartley, off the whaling ship *Star in the East,* in February 1891, who disappeared in the ocean while trying to harpoon a whale. When the whale was killed after three days, the missing sailor was found inside, unconscious, but alive. Other great fish, such as great white sharks, have been known to swallow not only men but horses.

We believe the Bible is the inspired Word of God and science only further shows its records as credible and trustworthy.

Jesus and Jonah

The account of Jonah also has the unimpeachable authority of none other than our Lord Himself. When the scribes and Pharisees hypocritically asked Jesus for a sign to certify His extraordinary claims, He answered, *But none will be given it except the sign of the Prophet Jonah. For as Jonah was three days and three nights in the belly of a huge fish, so the Son of Man will be three days and three nights in the heart of the earth. The men of Nineveh will stand up at the judgment with this generation and condemn it; for they repented at the preaching of Jonah, and now one greater than Jonah is here* (Matt. 12:39-41).

Jesus declared unequivocally that Jonah's deliverance from the belly of the great fish prefigured His own resurrection from the dead. As Jonah was entombed for three days in the fish and then miraculously delivered, so our Lord after three days in death's tomb was miraculously delivered by His mighty resurrection. Thus for one to deny the account of Jonah is to impeach the inspiration of Scripture and the word of our Lord Himself.

Jonah's Prayer

Man's extremity is God's opportunity! Let us beware of the pitfall of trying so much to see what was in the fish that we forget to see the drama happening within Jonah. The true miracle took place, not in the belly of the fish but in the heart of the prophet; not in the realm of nature, but in the realm of grace.

Entombed in the fish and in the depths of the sea, Jonah prayed: *In my distress I called to the Lord, and He answered me. From the depths of the grave I called for help, and You listened to my cry.* He graphically describes the horrors of being engulfed by water and having seaweed wrapped around his head. He exclaims, *but You brought my life up from the pit, O Lord my God* (Jonah 2:2-6).

It was only when Jonah looked away from himself and to God that he was delivered. At the end of his prayer he affirmed, *Salvation comes from the Lord* (v. 9). Then, and only then, the Lord commanded the fish to vomit Jonah onto dry land (v. 10).

Forgive me Lord, for my tendency to be distracted by the busyness of life so as not to hear Your voice, and for my lack of courage so as not to obey. Make me both a hearer and doer of Your Word.

83

God of the Second Chance

Read Jonah 3–4

Then the word of the Lord came to Jonah a second time (3:1). Ours is the God of the second chance. If you have any doubts, ask Moses, David, Peter, Mark. Who of us would have been able to stand were it otherwise? How many times have we failed and still God's grace has restored and recommissioned us?

Revival

Jonah must have been a strange sight. Having been embalmed in the gastric juices of the fish for three days, his skin was a strange color, his hair all white, looking like one who had returned from the dead. His strange appearance no doubt helped convince the Ninevites that his was no "fish tale."

Jonah obeyed, went to Nineveh, and faithfully preached his eight-word sermon. *Forty more days and Nineveh will be destroyed* (v. 4). The result was a great revival, perhaps the greatest mass revival in history. The king put aside his royal robes, dressed in sackcloth, and issued a proclamation of fasting and repentance for everyone in the kingdom. God had compassion and spared them.

Ironically we find Jonah displeased and angry, asking God to take his life. He could not accept God's forgiveness and favor toward the enemy nation of Nineveh.

And the sovereign God who had sent the tempest and had sent the fish now sends a worm to wither the vine that shelters the petulant prophet. God further sends a scorching east wind—perhaps the notorious sirocco—and the blazing sun causes Jonah to grow faint. He laments the withering of the vine as he clutches his nationalistic and racial exclusiveness. God chides him for being concerned about the vine but unconcerned about the people of Nineveh.

The God of Miracles

If we feel we have been "swallowed alive" by our circumstance, if we are discouraged, disheartened, or defeated, let us remember that He is still the God of miracles and wonders. If the story of Jonah's failure finds an echo in your heart, remember that He is the God of the second chance, and the second hundredth chance.

As someone has expressed it, every one of us is either in the caravan to Nineveh or on the boat to Tarshish. We are either going God's way, or going our own way. May we be obedient to the word of the Lord and be faithful witnesses wherever He may lead us.

God of the second chance, and of the second hundredth chance, thank You for loving me and saving me in spite of my failures.

M I C A H

A Ballad of Doom

84

A Tale of Two Cities

Read Micah 1

MICAH WAS A SON OF THE SOIL, a peasant turned prophet. His family was obscure, his town was small, his book is termed minor, but his message is mighty. His fiery sermons thundered against business, government, and religious leaders for their corruption and oppression of the poor. His preachment culminates with some of the most extraordinary and best known texts in the Bible.

A Tale of Two Cities

Micah shares *the vision he saw concerning Samaria and Jerusalem.* God gave him an x-ray vision of the society in which he lived. He saw through the veneer of success and religious ritual and perceived how the powerful exploited the poor with illegal interest rates, foreclosures, and debt slavery. His words burn with indignation as he sees his neighboring farmer friends defrauded by the rich.

Micah is not a prophet who writes from an armchair

position. He pronounces judgment with a broken heart as he goes about barefooted and stripped of his upper garment. His wails are like the terrifying night call of the jackal and his howls as the sad moan of the owl. His prophetic expression of fear and grief for God's judgment to come is given, not in sternness, but in anguish as he laments for *my people* (1:8-9).

I will make Samaria a heap of rubble (v. 6) is his prophecy of doom against the capital of Israel. This was fulfilled in Micah's lifetime when in 721 B.C. Samaria was destroyed by the Assyrian armies. His judgment against Samaria and Jerusalem (vv. 3-7) was further fulfilled when in 701 Jerusalem and Judah were overrun by King Sennacherib and his army.

From Plowman to Penman

Though he was a tiller of the soil and rough man of the country, through the inspiration of the Holy Spirit Micah rose to eloquent heights, with some of his verses becoming classics. All but the first verse of his book is written in poetry. In his ballad of Samaria's demise he portrays the Lord treading the mountains as His steppingstones with the earth becoming a level plain under His majestic stride (vv. 3-4).

For the coming judgment upon Judah he uses in sharp satire a series of puns on the towns' names (vv. 10-15). The *Phillips* translation best brings out this play on their implicit meaning:

> *So then, in Gath where tales are told, breathe not a word! In Acco, the town of Weeping, shed no tear! In Aphrah, the house of Dust, grovel in the dust! And you who live in Shaphir, the Beauty—town, Move on, for your shame lies naked! You who live in Zaanan, the town of Marching, There is no marching for you now!*

We must each give an account for ourselves on God's Day of Judgment. We then will either hear the sweet words, "Well done," or the thundering sentence, "Depart, you cursed." God's warnings are somber and sacred. Let us take heart and heed them.

HELP ME GOD, TO LIVE IN LIGHT OF AND PREPARATION FOR JUDGMENT DAY.

85

A Ballad of Doom

Read Micah 2–3

THE FIRST THREE CHAPTERS of Micah compose a ballad of denouncement and doom. In vigorous language and graphic imagery Micah rebukes the rampant corruption and oppression of the poor. He describes the oppressors as those who covet others' land and houses and seize them, defrauding man of his home and inheritance (2:1). They *plan iniquity* (v. 1) but God is *planning disaster* against them (v. 3), with punishment that suits their crimes. Their heinous crimes are graphically described as social cannibalism (3:1-3). The corrupt religious leaders who have turned religion into a greedy enterprise will be forsaken by God (vv. 5-12).

The Late Great Nation U.S.A.

We too were a nation founded upon righteousness. The founders of this nation came to these shores in quest of religious freedom. They legislated for each session of Congress to open with prayer and inscribed upon our coins, "In

God We Trust." Our first president knelt in the snows of Valley Forge to seek guidance and strength.

But we too have strayed far from those principles. We have outlawed prayer in our schools, made legal the killing of innocent unborn children, and spawned a generation victimized by drugs, AIDS, and the specter of a nuclear holocaust. We have placed our trust in GNP and have forgotten the One who brought us out of our Egypt.

Perhaps the Book of Micah is a tale of three cities: of Samaria, Jerusalem, and the city in which we live! From the pages of God's Word, the Lord calls out to us as a nation, *Listen! The Lord is calling to the city* (6:9).

GOD OF OUR FATHERS, BLESS OUR NATION WITH RIGHTEOUSNESS, JUSTICE, COMPASSION, AND A FIRM FAITH, KNOWING THAT YOU ALONE ARE OUR SOURCE OF GOODNESS AND GREATNESS.

86

A World Text

Read Micah 4

Micah proclaimed God's message on Jerusalem's Wall Street of his day, in the places of commerce, government, and religion. He denounced the officials for their corruption, the land-grabbers for their oppression, and the religious leaders for fleecing instead of feeding the flock.

This anthology of Micah's prophecies alternates between gloom and glory, destruction and deliverance. Micah through the ages has been remembered primarily for his glowing texts of God's precious promises of peace and blessing to come.

A World Text

In the 1949 Cultural Revolution in China The Salvation Army was disbanded and Major Hung Shun Yin with others was forced to work in the labor camps. For over thirty years he was incommunicado with the Christian world, disallowed a normal worship experience, and deprived of his pen as editor of our publications in China. But all through that time he kept alive his love of the Lord.

When in 1981 he came to the U.S.A. for the first time, there were three things he wanted to see as I was privileged to host him in New York, along with my friend Major Check Yee of San Francisco. Major Yin wanted to see the national headquarters of The Salvation Army, the Statue of Liberty, and the sculpture in front of the U.N. that has an inscription from Micah.

Major Yin was a son of war-torn China. The verse that this man who had come from the labor camps of communist China wanted to see that day, the one that held out to him God's shining promise, is from the Prophet Micah:

> *They will beat their swords into plowshares and their spears into pruning hooks. Nation will not take up sword against nation, nor will they train for war anymore* (4:3).

These words are virtually the same as recorded by Isaiah (2:4), a contemporary of Micah. When the nations of the earth formed their world organization, they chose these classic words to epitomize their hope that war and terror and violence would become a thing of the past.

Micah proclaims that "In the last days" this picture of harmony and peace will prevail. There is coming a day when war and oppression shall be no more, and *Every man will sit under his own vine and under his own fig tree, and no one will make them afraid* (Micah 4:4). The vine and fig tree were symbols of peace and security.

Let us, from this ancient text, take hope for the future. God's loving purpose for man will not be aborted. Wars and violence and sin will ultimately be ended and God's peace shall reign. Let us so live as to be a part of God's eternal kingdom of peace and joy and blessing indescribable.

HEAVENLY FATHER, LEAD ME INTO YOUR CREATIVE PURPOSE FOR MY LIFE THAT I MAY SOMEDAY LIVE AND REIGN WITH YOU FOREVER.

87

MICAH'S CHRISTMAS TEXT

READ MICAH 5

CHRISTMAS EACH YEAR WEAVES its magic spell upon our hearts. Carols float on the air and there is a surge of love and kindliness not felt at any other time of the year. Creches appear reminding us of the miracle in the manger. In that feeding trough in lowly Bethlehem, a cry from that Infant's throat broke the centuries of silence. For the first time God's voice could be heard coming from human vocal cords. C.S. Lewis called that event—the coming of Christ at Christmas—"the greatest rescue mission of history."

During each Christmas season the words of Micah resonate throughout the world. For he was inspired to give the prophecy that named the very birthplace of the Messiah: *But you, Bethlehem Ephrathah, though you are small among the clans of Judah, out of you will come for Me one who will be ruler over Israel, whose origins are from of old, from ancient times* (5:2).

Micah was telling those who were proud and powerful

and rich and self-righteous that God's great ruler would not come from their stately and royal environs. He would come forth from the nondescript hamlet of Bethlehem. When over 700 years later the wise men came searching for Him, the scribes had to brush off the dust from the Book of Micah to direct them to the very location where He would be born.

The One who would come is One *whose origins are from of old, from ancient times* (v. 2). This literally means "from days of eternity." It speaks of the eternal existence of Christ. His providence and preeminence are also prophesied as one who *will stand and shepherd His flock and His greatness will reach to the ends of the earth. And He will be their peace* (vv. 4-5). What beautiful and precious promises are ours from this plowman who became God's mighty penman.

CHRIST OF THE BETHLEHEM MANGER, I WOULD MAKE ROOM FOR YOU TO BE BORN IN THE LOWLY MANGER OF MY HEART, AND THERE TO LIVE AND LOVE AND WORK THROUGH ME.

88

WHAT THE LORD REQUIRES

READ MICAH 6–7

MICAH POSES THE PIVOTAL question for our lives: *what does the Lord require of you?* Our destiny for this life and the next hangs in the balance in our answer to that question. There is no question more important for us to know and answer rightly.

Micah gives the answer to this question. Some of his day thought the Lord's requirements of them were in the rituals they performed. But Micah tells the Israelites that it is not their burnt offerings or their rituals that God desires from them (6:6-7). God's requirement for each of us is not found in our religious rites and rituals. God's plowman turned prophet cuts a deeper furrow to let his hearers know the meaning of true religion.

Micah probes their convictions: *He has showed you, O man, what is good. And what does the Lord require of you?* (v. 8) What does the Lord require of us? God through His prophet gives the answer in a text that has become one of the towering mountain peaks of the Bible. In this classic text God gives us His definition for true religion in a single terse statement. *To act justly and to love mercy and to walk humbly with your God* (v. 8).

"To act justly" speaks of honesty, integrity, uprightness; of being incorrupt, ethical, truthful. Disraeli defined justice as "truth in action." Our world of duplicity and rampant corruption cries out for justice, for truth in action.

"To love mercy" speaks of kindness, compassion, forgiveness, love, tenderness. Our world and people around us desperately need these qualities. Shakespeare reminds us in his *Merchant of Venice* that "The quality of mercy . . . is twice blest; It blesseth him that gives and him that takes."

In God's trilogy of requirements He takes us from the horizontal to the vertical relationship and calls us "to walk humbly with your God." It declares the essence of what our faith is all about. Our faith is not a ritual, it is a relationship. To walk with God—what a priceless privilege! To walk with God—what a sacred responsibility!

The Incomparable God

Who is a God like you? asks Micah (7:18). Indeed He is the incomparable God who pardons sin, shows compassion, and fulfills His precious promises (vv. 18-20). Then Micah flings out a text that has assured the heart of many a reclaimed sinner. God not only forgives our sins, He casts them away forever. Micah, choosing a metaphor that selects the most inaccessible and unretrievable place he could think of, declares, God will *hurl all our iniquities into the depths of the sea* (v. 19).

The mighty message of this great prophet aptly closes in this paean of praise. May we, in our world of change and crisis, share his hope and affirm with him: *But as for me, I watch in hope for the Lord, I wait for God my Savior* (v. 7).

Lord God, how great You are, how small are we; how infinite is Your wisdom, how limited is ours; how mighty You are, how weak we are; how holy are Your ways, how selfish are ours. Touch us with Your transforming power to fashion us after Your will.

N A H U M

"Lest We Forget"

89

"Lest We Forget"

Read Nahum 1–3

The winds of war blow through the Book of Nahum and its theme is one of violence and vengeance. We can only understand this book if we journey into Nahum's world and know something about Nineveh, the object of God's vengeance and destruction.

A Refuge in the Storm

The one radiant promise of this book declares: *The Lord is good, a refuge in times of trouble. He cares for those who trust in Him* (1:7). True, He will punish the unrepentant sinner, but He will be the security of the believer. Martin Luther, in the dangerous days of the Reformation, found comfort in this verse. Nahum's very name meant "comfort" and in the midst of destruction around them God brings comfort to His people.

The End of Nineveh

In dramatic contrast with God's care for His people, the

prophet delivers the burden of his message: *But with an overwhelming flood He will make an end of Nineveh* (v. 8). To us this statement has little impact. But to those who heard it from Nahum, it was a staggering pronouncement.

Nineveh was the largest and most magnificent city of history at that time. It was the capital of Assyria. It boasted eight miles of defensive wall with 1,200 towers and fourteen fortified gates, up to sixty feet high and wide enough for several chariots to race abroad. The city was further protected by a great moat, seeming to make it impregnable. Israel and that part of the world knew all too well the oppressive heel of Assyria on its back. Nahum's reference to "an overwhelming flood" that would make an end of Nineveh is exactly what historians tell us brought doom to this most fortified city of the ancient world.

Nahum prophesied that the destruction would be so complete that *you will have no descendants to bear your name* (v. 14). So precisely was this fulfilled that for almost two and a half millenniums no one even knew the site of this renowned city. Only in the last century have excavations brought to light the ruins of a vast metropolis that correspond with the declarations of Jonah and Nahum of the magnificence of this city and its destruction at the zenith of its pomp and glory. How perfectly accurate are the prophecies of God's Word.

The second chapter of Nahum is considered a masterpiece for its graphic portrayal of military assault. Nahum's poetic prediction is unsurpassed for vivid description and poetic fervor of the siege of the world's most magnificent city. Its often staccato lines convey the sense and sound of the chaos and conflict: *Guard the fortress, watch the road, brace yourselves, marshal all your strength* (2:1).

The text throbs with graphic war scenes—*Chariots storm through the streets . . . flashing swords and glittering spears . . . hearts melt, knees give way . . . the clatter of wheels, galloping horses and jolting chariots, charging caval-*

ry. Doom and death dominate with piles of dead, bodies without number, people stumbling over the corpses (2:4–3:3).

God charges that Nineveh was *the city of blood, full of lies, full of plunder, never without victims!* (3:1) The chronicles of Assyrian King Ashurbanipal II tell of his own atrocities upon those taken captive, including skinning commanders alive, impaling on stakes, gouging out eyes, and cutting off limbs of officers and boasting "with their blood I dyed the mountain red like wool." The fiendish cruelty of the Assyrians was without parallel in the ancient world.

Nothing can heal your wound; your injury is fatal (v. 19). Earlier Nineveh repented under the preachment of Jonah and was temporarily spared. But their return to even more heinous sins put them beyond hope. Little could the powerful kings of Assyria know that their vassal Jerusalem would flourish long after the glory and grandeur of Nineveh had become a heap of ruins, buried in the sands of time.

Rudyard Kipling was chosen to write a poem of celebration for the diamond jubilee of Queen Victoria. It was 1897 and the British Empire was at its apex of power. He had a difficult time composing a poem for the occasion but finally came up with his *Recessional* that baffled and angered many:

Lo, all our pomp of yesterday
Is one with Nineveh and Tyre!
Judge of the Nations, spare us yet,
Lest we forget—lest we forget!

Let us as individuals and as a nation hear and heed the message of Nahum, "Lest we forget." Let us remember the timeless truth of God's Word that *righteousness exalts a nation, but sin is a disgrace to any people* (Prov. 14:34).

HOLY GOD, KEEP OUR NATION MINDFUL OF YOUR PROVIDENCE IN OUR BEGINNINGS, AND YOUR RIGHTEOUSNESS, LEST WE FORGET.

Living by Faith

90

Living by Faith

Read Habakkuk 1–2

Habakkuk, though one of the most brief books, is one of the most mighty and memorable books of the Old Testament. Its towering truth became a landmark of New Testament theology and altered the course of spiritual and church history. The book is unique in that it is not addressed to Israel but rather is a dialogue between the prophet and God.

The Problem

The prophet commences with an anguished complaint that has a very contemporary ring: *Destruction and violence are before me; there is strife, and conflict abounds . . . justice is perverted* (1:3-4). He poses questions that every thoughtful believer must at some time confront. Why does God seem not to answer prayer? (v. 2) Why does God tolerate injustice and wrong? (v. 3) His tormented soul over the violence and injustice around him leads him to question whether God cares or is in control.

What he then hears from God only further deepens his perplexity. Discipline and chastening are deserved but he is astonished that God will do it through the Chaldeans—a ruthless people. Their might is described in graphic terms (vv. 6-11). Habakkuk is then led to his second complaint: How could a holy God appoint such a godless and violent nation to execute His judgments (vv. 12-17), a God of whom the prophet says, *Your eyes are too pure to look on evil* (v. 13).

The Promise

The prophet goes to his watchtower—a tower on the city walls from which a watchman could keep a sharp eye out for an enemy—there to set himself apart and await God's answer to his prayer of desperation (2:1). It is a difficult discipline to wait on the Lord. Our restlessness and hyperactive spirits are not prone to stop and wait. But if we are to receive God's revelations we must ascend our watchtowers of prayer above the mist of earth's confusion and quietly wait upon God.

As he maintains his lonely watch, the Lord answers Habakkuk. The revelation He gives will be not only for the prophet but for all generations. Habakkuk is told to take up his stylus and set it forth plainly so heralds may run to proclaim it.

God gives to the prophet what is destined to become the watchword of Christianity, the central message of this mighty book—*The righteous will live by his faith* (v. 4). This towering truth was to become a foundation of theology of the New Testament, where it is quoted no less than three times.

The Apostle Paul cites this revelation from Habakkuk's watchtower as he declares in his theological treatise to Christians of all ages, *The righteous will live by faith* (Gal. 3:11). And when the author of the Book of Hebrews wanted to fling out the secret of traveling the pilgrim's pathway through this world, once again there is proclaimed the revelation given to

Habakkuk, this time as exemplified by the Lord Himself: *But My righteous one will live by faith* (Heb. 10:38).

Some years ago when we were touring Rome we entered the church of St. John's Lateran. In it is a marble staircase said to be the one Jesus ascended in Pilate's judgment hall. We witnessed the sight of pilgrims mounting it on their knees, a step at a time, saying prayers as they ascended. Centuries before a monk was performing this rite as he was seeking his salvation through works and rites of the church. What happened to Martin Luther on those stairs was recorded by his son: "As he repeated his prayers on the Lateran staircase, the words of the Prophet Habakkuk came suddenly to his mind: 'The just shall live by faith.' Thereupon he ceased his prayers, returned to Wittenberg, and took this as the chief foundation of all his doctrine."

In that moment, as the mighty truth of this text given to the Prophet Habakkuk gripped Luther's mind and soul, the Reformation was born that would sweep across Europe and spread throughout the world. Luther had found that it was not his good works but his faith in Christ that justified him. Luther himself testified: "When by the Spirit of God, I understood those words, 'the just shall live by faith!' then I felt born again like a new man; I entered the open door into the very paradise of God." This text from Habakkuk became the battle cry of the Reformation.

God would remind us once again through the timeless text of Habakkuk that it is only on the merit of the grace of our Lord Jesus Christ and our faith in Him that we are justified. It is not what we do for God that will get us into heaven, but what He has done for us, on Calvary.

LORD, INCREASE MY FAITH, FOR I HAVE NO MERIT OF MY OWN BUT LEAN WHOLLY ON YOUR LOVE AND SALVATION FOR ME.

91

The Prophet's Prayer

Read Habakkuk 3

The Presence in Prayer

The prophet comes into the presence of Jehovah in awe—*I stand in awe of Your deeds, O Lord* (3:2). He reminds us that we are not to come casually into the presence of the Creator of the universe. Our approach to prayer needs to be one of awe before the omnipotent and omniscient God.

Preceding his prayer is his declaration: *But the Lord is in His holy temple; let all the earth be silent before Him* (2:20). There is a sacred hush that befits the believer when we come into the presence of God.

To the prophet is vouchsafed a vision of the majestic God whose *splendor was like the sunrise* (3:4). As with all other persons in the Bible who were given a glimpse of the glory of God, Habakkuk is overwhelmed and records: *I heard and my heart pounded, my lips quivered at the sound; decay crept into my bones, and my legs trembled* (v. 16).

A Masterpiece of Affirmation

The prayer of the prophet closes with some of the most memorable and lyrical lines of Scripture. The story is told of Ben Franklin in Paris when he was mocked by some skeptics for his admiration of the Bible. One evening he entered their company with a manuscript that he said contained an ancient poem he had been reading and was impressed with its stately beauty. They asked him to share it with them and Franklin then read this great third chapter of Habakkuk, concluding with verses 17-19.

> *Though the fig tree does not bud and there are no grapes on the vines, though the olive crop fails and the fields produce no food, though there are no sheep in the pen and no cattle in the stalls, yet I will rejoice in the Lord, I will be joyful in God my Savior. The Sovereign Lord is my strength; He makes my feet like the feet of a deer, He enables me to go on the heights.*

The Praise and Power of Prayer

Habakkuk's prayer embraces the probable calamities that may befall as the ruthless Chaldeans are about to overrun his land and people. He anticipates the worst and in trust exclaims that though the crops fail, the flocks be destroyed, and the fields be barren, God would be his strength. Habakkuk's prayer is one of the most courageous expressions of trust in the Bible. God has led him from trial to triumph, from fear to faith.

Yet will I rejoice in the Lord is his ringing testimony. What eloquence is in that word, "yet." His rejoicing is not due to any "prosperity theology." God did not give him any "Seven Steps to Successful Living." Rather it is in the midst of failure and deprivation of all those things considered most essential to happiness that God enables the prophet to give voice to praise.

Surely, if in the twilight of past dispensation the prophet could triumph over the worst that life brought to him, how much more possible should it be for us who live in the blaze of the One who came to be the Light of the World! Let us with God's mighty penman of old testify: *The Sovereign Lord is my strength!*

GOD OF LOVE, WHEN DARK SHADOWS CROSS THE THRESHOLD OF MY LIFE, ILLUMINE MY PATH BY THE ONE WHO IS MY LIGHT AND SALVATION.

ZEPHANIAH

THE GREAT DAY OF THE LORD

92

THE GREAT DAY OF THE LORD

READ ZEPHANIAH 1–3

AN UNUSUAL SILENCE prevails in Old Testament prophecy for the first three quarters of the seventh century B.C. No prophetic voice is heard since the memorable utterances of Hosea, Amos, Micah, and Isaiah at the close of the eighth century B.C. Then as a phoenix the voice of Zephaniah emerges from the ashes of Judah's decadence and near demise.

THE BAD NEWS

No doubt many who heard Zephaniah would have preferred the silence. The prophet wasted no words on pleasantries or introductions. He gets right down to the burden of his message—divine judgment upon Judah's sin that will bring total devastation. *I will sweep away everything from the face of the earth* is his proclamation from the Lord, with the destruction to be total (1:2-3). His message becomes a summary of the pre-exilic prophets—the eight who with him prophesied before the Babylonian Exile.

The prophet flings out his mighty message as he proclaims, *The great Day of the Lord is near* (v. 14). The Day of the Lord or its equivalent is repeated no less than twenty times in this brief book. The horrors of the judgment of that day tumble from his lips as an avalanche of woes upon the nation: *That day will be a day of wrath, a day of distress and anguish, a day of trouble and ruin, a day of darkness and gloom, a day of clouds and blackness* (v. 15).

From this obscure prophet has come a hymn reputed to be translated in more languages than any other hymn. The apocalyptic message of 1:15 fired the imagination of Thomas of Celano, a thirteenth-century companion and biographer of St. Francis. The friar's famous hymn, "Dies Irae," is based on Zephaniah's prophecy of the day of the Lord and in English is rendered: *Days of wrath and doom impending, / . . . Heaven and earth in ashes ending.* The message of the hymn has carried over from its plainsong of medieval time and its use in the Requiem Mass to the enduring settings given by Mozart, Berlioz, Verdi, and others. How remarkably God preserves the message of those He calls to proclaim His ways and Word!

The Good News

But as with the other prophets, the message of doom is not the final word. There is good news indeed for those who *may call on the name of the Lord,* whom He *will purify* (3:9). There will be a remnant who will do God's will and rejoice (vv. 13-16). God's penman concludes with one of the most beautiful assurances in the prophetic tradition:

> *The Lord your God is with you, He is mighty to save. He will take great delight in you, He will quiet you with His love, He will rejoice over you with singing* (3:17).

From this little known book of the Old Testament comes an enduring message to all generations. First, God is sovereign. History and events are under His control and are working toward His ultimate design.

Second, God will not tolerate continued sin and is bringing a day of judgment that will be universal. A day of reckoning is coming for every soul. We will individually be confronted with the great Day of the Lord.

Third, the justice and plan of God will ultimately triumph over evil. Fourth, a remnant will be saved. To the prodigal nation comes the divine promise, *I will bring you home* (v. 20).

From the New Testament comes the challenge for our response to the inspired message of Zephaniah: *Since everything will be destroyed in this way, what kind of people ought you to be? You ought to live holy and godly lives as you look forward to the day of God and speed its coming* (2 Peter 3:11-12). Let us rise up to the challenge of holy living to be prepared for the grandest event of our lives.

LORD GOD, LET YOUR WISDOM INSTRUCT ME, YOUR STRENGTH PRESERVE ME, AND YOUR WILL DIRECT ME.

Desire of All Nations

93

"Give Careful Thought"

Read Haggai 1–2

"Give careful thought" could well be considered the theme of Haggai. No less than five times do we find this statement in his brief thirty-eight-verse, two-chapter book (1:5, 7; 2:15, 18 [twice]). "Consider your ways" is the rendering of the old *King James Version.* It is a summons to personal evaluation, a reordering of our priorities.

The Book of Ezra gives us the context of Haggai's ministry and message. The Persian Emperor Cyrus in 536 B.C. allowed Jewish exiles in Babylon to return to Jerusalem to rebuild the temple, a symbol of God's presence among the people. Some sixteen years later, the work lagged and the people were merely looking out for themselves. They had given in to the hardships and hostilities and forgotten about the Lord's house. Their neglect allowed to remain in ruins what once had been the pride of Israel.

Now in 520 B.C. God sends Haggai to call the people to *give careful thought to your ways.* Haggai tells them it is time to get on with the long-neglected job of rebuilding their place of worship. He calls the remnant amid the rubble to surmount their discouragement and return to moral greatness. He summons them from apathy to action.

"Give careful thought" is ever a contemporary message from God. He summons us to carefully consider our priorities. What place does God have in the everyday matters of our life? How is it in our home? In our business? In our devotional life? In our finances? In our physical life? In our relationships? Are our disciplines and priorities in order? Does God have first place in all these areas? Is it possible we have neglected the sacred for the secular, the pursuit of excellence for easy expedience?

The time has not yet come for the Lord's house to be built (v. 2) was the excuse of the people. Procrastination still robs us of doing God's will and work when it should be done. How many times have we heard or said: "I know I should get about that task, but right now I'm too busy." The road of "maybe someday" leads to the land of never.

With a touch of irony, God asks them, *Is it a time for you yourselves to be living in your paneled houses, while this house remains a ruin*? (v. 4) Still today when we plead we do not have time for God's priorities there is the same inconsistency. We find time for what we want, for what is most important to us personally. The problem is not time, it is priority. What is most important? The ordering of priorities requires that we do not live under the tyranny of the urgent to the neglect of the important.

The frantic and feverish activity of our day is echoed in Haggai's description of his hearers: *You have planted much, but have harvested little. You eat, but never have enough. You drink, but never have your fill* (v. 5). We are a restless people. Our culture has an insatiable desire for possessions and pleasures and can all too easily leave us in spiritual barrenness and poverty. *You earn wages, only to put them in a purse with holes in it* (v. 6) is a painful diagnosis of our day of runaway inflation and devaluation by taxes and government overspending. The ancient text of Haggai is close to where we live.

Haggai's message found a ready response. The people *obeyed the voice of the Lord their God and the message of the Prophet Haggai* (v. 12).

There comes the word: *"Be strong . . . and work. For I am with you," declares the Lord Almighty* (2:4). This designation for God is found fourteen times in this book, emphasizing that God's presence brings the power to accomplish our tasks.

The Desire of the Nations

The prophet is inspired to move from the practical needs at hand to the grand event of the ages—*the desired of all nations will come* (v. 7). Through the centuries this text has been looked upon as messianic, a promise of the One who alone can fulfill the deepest longings of all people and nations.

Handel's *Messiah* has further immortalized this text in the early part of his oratorio with Haggai's promise. *Thus saith the Lord of Hosts, yet once a little while and I will shake the heavens and the earth, the sea and the dry land, and I will shake all nations, and the desired of all nations shall come.* Yahweh was going to shake nations with an event that would have impact upon the world, and the future glory of this temple, composed of living stones, will surpass the former.

The title of our Lord given by Haggai caught the inspired imagination of Charles Wesley and led him to pen for all of us who are exiles far from home:

> *All Thy people's consolation, Hope of all the earth Thou art; Dear desire of every nation, Joy of every longing heart.*

HOLY GOD, HELP ME NOT TO LIVE UNDER THE TYRANNY OF THE URGENT, BUT TO KEEP MY PRIORITIES IN ORDER.

The King is Coming

94

Visions at Midnight

Read Zechariah 1–3

The Book of Zechariah is one of the most frequently quoted books in the New Testament. Its more than seventy references—with about a third of them in the Gospels and more than half in the Book of Revelation—underscores its importance in the Word of God. It hosts some of the most sacred messianic prophecies. Our Lord Himself identified with its prophetic passages.

Zechariah is one of the longest books of the minor prophets and the most difficult to understand. The scholar Jerome termed it "the most obscure of books." Nevertheless, it provides rich insights and pulsates with the ultimate hope of salvation in Christ.

Thirty different people in the Old Testament had the common name of Zechariah, meaning "The Lord remembers." The prophet reminded the people that the Lord remembers His promises and takes action to fulfill them. Zechariah, with Haggai, prophesied from about 520 to 480 B.C. during the Hebrews' return to their homeland following their captivity in

Babylon. Christ Himself identifies the prophet as having paid the high cost of martyrdom for this faithfulness, being murdered between the temple and the altar (Matt. 23:35).

"Return to Me," declares the Lord Almighty, "and I will return to you" (Zech. 1:3) is the burden of the prophet's message. The name *Yahweh,* translated "the Lord Almighty," is found no less than forty-one times throughout the book and was used by Zechariah to assure the Israelites that God keeps His promises. The prophet makes this lofty name the final word of his prophetic writing.

Zechariah's message was in part to encourage the people in the rebuilding of the temple. We too are often engaged in the rebuilding process. Sometimes it is the rebuilding of a life beset by tragedy or failure, or it may be the rebuilding of a church, community, or nation following change or crisis. If our work is to be more than a veneer to cover an inner sickness, it must include, as Zechariah reminds us, a return to the Lord, a total commitment to Him.

Visions at Midnight (1:7–6:15)

When darkness comes to a people, they need a vision of what God can do. Zechariah recorded eight memorable visions the Lord gave to him during the night of February 15, 519 B.C.

The first vision was of *The Man among the Myrtle Trees.* These trees are symbolic of Israel—not the stately cedars or strong oaks, but by the small and lowly myrtle trees that grow in the lowlands. The interpreting angel declares that the Lord will return to them with mercy and comfort. The compelling message for each of us is that, although we too are insignificant, the Lord is in the midst with grace for those faithful to Him.

Four Horns, the focus of the second vision, are empires that defeated and scattered God's people. But for each enemy, there is a Craftsman who will ultimately overcome the adversary. So God provides forces to overcome and shape to

His purpose the enemies of our soul (1:18-21).

The third vision of *A Man with a Measuring Line* (chap. 2) prophesies of the new and expanded Jerusalem, a city without walls that will include all nations and peoples. Here alone in Scripture is the designation *the holy land* for Jerusalem, given a deeper meaning by the life and ministry of Christ. All God's people will find a final home and rest in the Holy City. It is in this vision that God says of Israel, *Whoever touches you touches the apple of His eye* (2:8).

Clothed in New Garments, the fourth vision (chap. 3), presents a message of salvation. The high priest, representing the people, is seen in filthy clothes, symbolic of our moral defilement and unworthiness before a holy God. The Lord rebukes the accusation of Satan, declaring that the believer is as *a burning stick snatched from the fire* (v. 2). The filthy clothes are exchanged for clean garments, with the angel saying, *See, I have taken away your sin, and I will put rich garments on you* (v. 4).

In the last book of the Bible, John's magnificent vision of heaven portrays the believer as the bride of Christ clothed in new garments (Rev. 19:8). Our Lord, by His redemptive work, exchanges our soiled and sinful garb for His own robe of righteousness. He enables us to stand redeemed before His throne by the merit of His righteousness imputed to us.

In Zechariah's vision are the symbolic titles of the Lord, *Servant, Branch, Stone,* and the prophecy of our Lord's work on Calvary: *I will remove the sin of this land in a single day* (Zech. 3:9). Against the mighty atonement and intercession of Christ, no satanic charges can prevail. By the offering of Christ every believer is as "a brand plucked from the burning."

Heavenly Father, help me put Your will before mine, others before self, the things of the Spirit before the things of the body, the attainment of noble ends before pleasures.

95

Visions and Victory

Read Zechariah 4–8

The fifth of Zechariah's memorable midnight visions (chap. 4) depicts a gold lampstand arranged around a large bowl that serves as a bountiful reservoir of oil, with seven channels conveying the fuel to the seven lights. Here no human hand provides the oil but on each side is an olive tree with a continual flow for the light of the lampstand.

The lesson from the symbol of the candelabrum is that Israel—and later all believers—as God's lightbearers to the world, are sustained in their witness by the Holy Spirit, of whom oil is a symbol. Human resources are not adequate to accomplish God's tasks. *"Not by might nor by power, but by My Spirit," says the Lord Almighty* (4:6). Our witness and light to the world is sustained only by the Holy Spirit.

The sixth vision of *The Flying Scroll* and seventh of *The Woman in a Basket* have to do with judgment (chap. 5). They depict the universal curse of sin. The eighth and final vision of the *Four Chariots and Horses* speak also of God's sovereignty in history. In His own way and time God sends forth His chariots to accomplish His purpose. The passage of history is not a random process but moves toward His ultimate design.

The Coronation

In a symbolic act, a crown is set on the head of the high priest, signifying the one *whose name is Branch, and He will branch out from His place and build the temple of the Lord . . . and He will be clothed with majesty and will sit and rule on His throne. And He will be a Priest on His throne . . . Those who are far away will come and help to build the temple of the Lord.*

Branch is one of the titles for Christ in Scripture. This messianic text prophesies Christ coming as King and Priest to set up His universal kingdom of righteousness and peace. This positive appendage to the visions of Zechariah makes a fitting climax to the end of the first division of this book, presenting a telescopic look down the centuries of God's grand design.

Call for Authentic Faith (chap. 7)

A deputation came to ask if, now that the temple had been rebuilt, it were still necessary to fast on the fast day that had been added during the Captivity to mark the sad time of Jerusalem's fall and the destruction of the temple. The Lord answered their question with a question: *Was it really for Me that you fasted?* (7:5) It was a rebuke for what started out as a meaningful memorial but had become a mere ritual.

Why does one observe a ceremonial practice? All religious practices are not ends in themselves, but a means to an end. They should lead us to a closer understanding and walk with God and render us more useful for His service.

Our text challenges us to ask, "What is our motive and attitude in our religious forms and practice?" Let us beware lest our religious ceremonies become empty rituals, hollow exercise, legal drudgery. Let us beware lest our religious practice be a mechanical going-through-the-motions, which misses the dynamics of its purpose. Let us beware lest our observances become self-serving instead of God-honoring. God calls us to an authentic faith and practice.

Zechariah emphasizes that ritual without obedience to the ethical demands of God's law is futile. All of life needs to be sacramental. Albert Orsborn eloquently expressed that truth in his song:

My life must be Christ's broken bread,
My love His outpoured wine,
A cup o'erfilled, a table spread
Beneath His name and sign,
That other souls, refreshed and fed,
May share His life through mine.

The New Jerusalem

Zechariah advocates that the fasts about which the people asked be turned into festivals, their mourning into mirth, and their ceremonies into celebration.

His prophetic vision takes the people beyond the ruins and rebuilding of the present city to the New Jerusalem. The city did not at the time host many elderly because of the Babylonian Captivity, but the new city will be peopled with senior citizens who will enrich the community by their presence and wisdom. Unlike the current setting, there will be heard the gleeful echo of children playing in the streets. Worldwide evangelism will be a hallmark of the rejuvenated city.

The prophet uses his favorite term, *The Lord Almighty,* eighteen times in the eighth chapter, underscoring the omnipotent God standing behind and fulfilling His promises.

HELP US, DEAR LORD, TO EVER BE HUMBLE IN SELF-ESTIMATE, AVERSE TO SELF-SEEKING, AND READY FOR SELF-SACRIFICE.

96

The Coming King

Read Zechariah 9–10

The Book of Zechariah divides into two parts. This second division, believed to be a later writing of the prophet, breathes a different air from that of the first eight chapters. Both the tone and content take a different cast.

The martial poetry of the first eight verses, which alternates throughout this second part of the book, vividly describes the pain and misery of war. Many expositors consider this text to refer to Alexander the Great. It prophesies, among other cities, the destruction of Tyre, that proud and pompous city, the New York of the ancient world. Tyre had successfully resisted the five-year siege of Shalmaneser of Assyria, and the thirteen-year siege of Nebuchadnezzar. But Alexander the Great conquered and destroyed this proud city in seven months.

With Judah in his path, Alexander marched to conquer it. But he had a strange dream of Israel's high priest coming out to meet him. This actually occurred as the Grecian king approached Jerusalem. By this divine intervention, he was led to spare the city. Indeed the prophecy was miraculously fulfilled, *But I will defend My house against marauding forces* (9:8).

But war will ultimately give way to peace. *Rejoice greatly, O Daughter of Zion* (v. 9) is the prophet's message. In contrast to the proud Alexander there will come another: *See, your King comes to you, righteous and having salvation, gentle and riding on a donkey, on a colt, the foal of a donkey.*

This text has become indelibly interwoven with the triumphal entry of our Lord as He, at the start of His passion week, came into Jerusalem riding on a donkey. The Gospel writers identify the Lord's entry to the city that day as the remarkable fulfillment of Zechariah's prophecy (Matt. 21:4-5; John 12:14-15).

The acclamation accorded our Lord that Palm Sunday was an oasis experience in the desert journey of the Man of Sorrows, the momentary recognition of His greatness, the one experience where earth paid homage to its true King. Palm branches, not spears, would be His escort. The songs of children, not the shouts of soldiers, would be His welcome. In contrast to Alexander and earth's kings, instead of war: *He will proclaim peace to the nations* (Zech. 9:10).

Alexander's "world conquests" will pale before the One of whom the prophet says: *His rule will extend from sea to sea and from the River to the ends of the earth* (v. 10).

Poet Charles Ross Weeds compares the two conquerors:

Jesus and Alexander both died at thirty-three.
One lived and died for self; one died for you and me.
The Greek died on a throne; the Jew died on a cross.
One's life a triumph seemed; the other but a loss.

One led vast armies forth; the other walked alone.
One shed a whole world's blood; the other gave His own.

Jesus and Alexander died at thirty-three.
One died in Babylon, and one on Calvary.
One gained all for himself; and one Himself He gave.
One conquered every throne; the other every grave.
The one made himself God, the God made Himself less.
The one lived to blast, the other but to bless.
When died the Greek, forever fell his throne of swords;
But Jesus died to live forever Lord of lords.

Jesus and Alexander died at thirty-three.
The Greek made all men slaves; the Jew made all men free.
One built a throne on blood; the other built on love.
The one was born of earth, the other from above.
One won all this earth, to lose all earth and heaven.
The other gave up all, that all to Him be given.
The Greek forever died; the Jew forever lives.
He loses all who gets, and wins all things who gives.

Our world today, as in the prophet's time, is marred by violence and war. War remains a perpetual companion of humankind. But there is One whom, when we invite Him to ascend the throne of our heart, brings peace in the midst of conflict, joy in the midst of distress. We rejoice in the hope of the prophet's message that ultimately *the Lord will appear* (9:14). The coming King will usher in a universal age of peace. And with another who was given the prophetical vision, we would pray, *Amen. Come, Lord Jesus* (Rev. 22:20).

Zechariah prophesies, *From Judah will come the cornerstone* (Zech. 10:4). Centuries later the Apostle Paul would declare that believers are "built on the foundation of the apostles and prophets, with Christ Jesus Himself as the chief cornerstone." Indeed, Christ is the foundation of our lives and all that will endure through eternity.

LORD GOD, GRANT TO ME THIS DAY SOME NEW VISION OF YOUR TRUTH AND MAKE ME A SOURCE OF STRENGTH TO SOMEONE IN NEED.

97

The Fountain Opened

Read Zechariah 11–14

Thirty Pieces of Silver

This chapter prophesies the betrayal of Christ for thirty pieces of silver. First it is the Lord who speaks: *So they paid me thirty pieces of silver. And the Lord said to me, "Throw it to the potter"—the handsome price at which they priced me.*

The prophet then acts out what Judas would do after he betrayed Jesus: *So I took the thirty pieces of silver and threw them into the house of the Lord to the potter* (11:12-13).

All this we see fulfilled to the letter in the betrayal of Jesus. He was sold for thirty pieces of silver; the betrayer cast the money down in the house of the Lord; in blind obedience to the Word, the chief priests gave it to the potter as the purchase price for a field in which to bury strangers (Matt. 27:3-10).

"On That Day"

And the God who is the source of Creation also has the power to move the created world toward its consummation.

No less than fifteen verses in the final three chapters begin with the words, *On that day*. The note of apocalyptic prophecy is dominant, and interpretation is hard to come by. One expositor calls these chapters "a 'pep talk' to the faithful and a nightmare to the sober expositor."

"That day" refers to the end times, the day to which all history inexorably moves. Mighty armies will be gathered against Jerusalem (Zech. 12:3). In striking imagery Zechariah describes God as defeating all the enemies of the faithful (vv. 4-9).

The One They Have Pierced

The veil will be taken away and in great contrition, *They will look on Me, the One they have pierced* (v. 10). The word "look" means to contemplate, seriously consider. His pierced hands and side, His wounds for their trangressions, His stripes for their healing, now become intensely impressed upon them. The Good Shepherd, whom they had rejected and slain, becomes the object of their grief and repentance that will know no bounds (vv. 10-13).

A Fountain Will Be Opened

On the prophet's broad canvas of epochal events to come, he portrays a striking and sacred scene: *On that day a fountain will be opened . . . to cleanse them from sin and impurity* (13:1). Indeed, an everflowing, purifying fountain of forgiveness and salvation was opened at Calvary. Its flowing waters have brought healing and health to an innumerable company who have plunged into its life-giving stream.

But this fountain was purchased at a high cost. In response to the question, *"What are these wounds on Your body?" He will answer, "The wounds I was given at the house of My friends"* (v. 6). The wounded one is described as the smitten shepherd (v. 7) in words that are directly quoted in the Gospel narrative of our Lord's passion (Matt. 27:31).

Zechariah's "Seismograph"

A news magazine reported that a large hotel chain sent a crew of engineers and geologists to Jerusalem to explore the possibility of building a hotel on top of the Mount of Olives. The scientists reported the site is the center of a geological fault, subject to earthquake. Another reported an oil company did seismic studies in quest of oil in the area. This survey discovered a gigantic fault running east and west through the center of the Mount of Olives, a fault so severe it could split at any time.

Zechariah did not know about seismographs, Richter scales, or the modern technology of geology. But he recorded his message from the One who made the mountains, rocks, and faults millenniums in advance to be ready for His coming! This remarkable prophecy of Zechariah declares: *On that day His feet will stand on the Mount of Olives, east of Jerusalem, and the Mount of Olives will be split in two from east to west* (14:4). Our Lord's glorious return will be at the same spot from which He left earth at His ascension (Acts 1:11-12).

On that day, after Armageddon, the Lord will have returned in mighty triumph and set up His kingdom. On that day *HOLY TO THE LORD will be inscribed on the bells of the horses, and the cooking pots in the Lord's house will be like the sacred bowls in front of the altar* (Zech. 14:20). In the new kingdom of God every distinction between the holy and the profane will be eliminated. The commonplace will be sacred, with ordinary cooking utensils used as vessels in the temple.

May we so live as to be ready to enter into His eternal kingdom of peace and holiness.

DEAR SAVIOR, THANK YOU FOR THE FOUNTAIN OF SALVATION OPENED AT CALVARY, FOR ITS SAVING AND PURIFYING WATERS.

MALACHI

THE LAST WORD

98

WHEN LOVE IS FORGOTTEN

READ MALACHI 1–2

"I HAVE LOVED YOU," *says the Lord* is the opening message of this last book of the Old Testament. God does not allow the oracles of the prophets to close without once more affirming His unchangeable love for His people.

Although they were faithless, He remains faithful. Malachi quotes God as declaring, *I the Lord do not change* (3:6). God is the same today as He was a billion years ago. He will always be sovereign. He will always be just. He will always be holy. He will always be omnipotent and omniscient. He will always be loving. Though we may fail and falter, God's love for us is unchanging. One of God's greatest and most assuring attributes is His immutability.

But the Israelites' high hope for the vanished glory of the days of David's reign had given way to the frustration of the postexilic age. The end of the Babylonian Captivity spurred hopes of ushering in the Messianic Age prophesied by earlier prophets. But only a remnant had returned and the new Jewish district was but a backwater station in the mighty Persian

Empire. A once virile religion had become humdrum. Such is the setting to which God called Malachi. His book could well be titled, "God's Message for a Discouraged People." It was an effort to rekindle the fires of a faith that had gone out.

Thus, with a touch of impudence, they ask of Jehovah, *How have You loved us?* (1:2) In other words, "If You really loved us, You would not let these things happen to us." They looked for worldly prosperity and glory as proof of His love.

This key word, "How," or its equivalent, recurs seven times in the debating style of this short book. Malachi's message does not come from the cloistered study but was hammered out in the verbal conflicts and debates of the marketplace, where assertions had to be defended against cynical objections. Seven times his hearers throw this rebuttal, "How?" at the prophet, denying his statements of God's love and their corruption.

Love is ever in danger of being taken for granted. A husband can take for granted the faithful love of a wife and an otherwise endearing relationship becomes casual and careless. A grown child can forget the sacrificial and devoted love of a parent and spurn that love with casual indifference. The people of Israel became blind to the love of God and in the process the light in their hearts turned to darkness.

Their apathy led them to bring blemished sacrifices in worship (vv. 6-14). Spiritual leaders violated their covenant. They had proved recreant in their sacred trust and became stumbling blocks instead of teachers for the people (vv. 1-9). Moral laxity, indifference, and skepticism were rampant.

William Booth's biographer tells how, near the end of Booth's life, the movement into which he had poured his soul and devotion began to be torn by rivalries, the most poignant within his own family. As his wife Catherine lay dying, her heart saddened by this turn of events, she said to her daughter, "Katie, why is it that God can't keep a thing pure for more than a generation?" (Ervine, *God's Soldier, II,* 841)

Malachi warns us of the peril of a once virile faith degenerating into a hollow and perfunctory ritual, with the followers of a heritage going mechanically about what once was a holy calling.

God Hates Divorce

"I hate divorce," says the Lord God (2:16) in one of the strongest passages in the Bible on the sanctity of marriage. The marriage vow is the most sacred and solemn commitment a person can make. In Malachi's time, the sanctity of marriage had eroded.

In an age that has popularized infidelity and divorce, that takes casually the violation of the marriage covenant, we need to hear anew God's standard for marriage, tucked away here in the ancient Book of Malachi: *The Lord is acting as the witness between you and the wife of your youth, because you have broken faith with her, though she is your partner, the wife of your marriage covenant. Has not the Lord made them one? In flesh and spirit they are His. . . . So guard yourself in your spirit, and do not break faith with the wife of your youth. "I hate divorce," says the Lord God of Israel* (vv. 14-16).

Never have Malachi's words on the sanctity of marriage been more needed. True, God in His Word specifies conditions where divorce is justified—infidelity and desertion (Matt. 5:32; 1 Cor. 7:15), but He calls us to fidelity in the sacred covenant of marriage and life partnership.

Heavenly Father, I would be true, for there are those who trust me. Keep me faithful to life's sacred covenants, and keep me faithful to life's tender and trusting relationships.

99

Last of the Prophets

Read Malachi 3

The Forerunner

"See, I will send *My messenger, who will prepare the way before Me. Then suddenly the Lord you are seeking will come to His temple; the messenger of the covenant, whom you desire, will come," says the Lord Almighty* (3:1). Here we have the remarkable prophecy of John the Baptist as the forerunner of Christ, the herald of the Messiah, who prepared the way before Him (Matt. 11:10).

This prophecy is amplified at the close of the book: *See, I will send you the Prophet Elijah before that great and dreadful Day of the Lord comes* (Mal. 4:5). Jesus, in citing this passage, drew the parallel between Elijah and John the Baptist in fulfillment of this prophecy (Matt. 17:10-13).

The Refiner's Fire

Malachi then announces that the coming of the Lord will be a time of judgment: *But who can endure the day of His coming? Who can stand when He appears? For He will be like a refiner's fire or a launderer's soap* (Zech. 3:2). These words have been further immortalized in Handel's *Messiah.*

At our Lord's return we will each be accountable. Indeed, it will be as the prophet has termed it, "a great and dreadful day." The judgment of God will be as an unquenchable fire.

Malachi announces that God's judgment will be as a refiner's fire and launderer's soap to purify His people. A refiner knows that his metal is pure when he can see his own image reflected in the mirrorlike surface of the metal after all the dross has been removed. God's work of grace will be completed when on that great day He will see His image restored and we are transformed into the very likeness of Christ.

Robbing God

God makes the startling charge that the people have robbed Him. Once again we hear the Israelites disputing the prophet's word, *How do we rob You?* God replies, *In tithes and offerings*. Then the familiar promise is given: *"Bring the whole tithe into the storehouse, that there may be food in My house. Test Me in this," says the Lord Almighty, "and see if I will not throw open the floodgates of heaven and pour out so much blessing that you will not have room enough for it"* (vv. 8-10).

The Israelites were holding back their required full tithe, 10 percent of their income, to God. Tithing was enjoined in the Mosaic Code of Deuteronomy (Deut. 14:23) and in the priestly code (Num. 18). This was the means by which the community maintained the temple, priesthood, and religious institutions. Faithful stewardship is still a requirement for the believer and still will crown the life with bountiful blessings.

Heavenly Father, whose mercies are new every morning, teach me to show my love to You by a faithful stewardship.

100

THE SUN OF RIGHTEOUSNESS

READ MALACHI 4

THE VERY LAST WORD of the Old Testament is curse. The prophets have pronounced a great day of judgment and the curse that is upon sin. But with judgment comes a brilliant ray that breaks through and gives a glorious hope for all humankind.

Malachi closes the Old Testament with one of the most radiant promises of the Bible: *But for you who revere My name, the sun of righteousness will rise with healing in its wings. And you will go out and leap like calves released from the stall* (4:2).

What the sun is to the earth, Christ is to the soul. The sun is our source of light, life, and beauty. Christ dispels darkness and diffuses His radiant light throughout the world and in the heart of man. Christ is our source of life and His beauty becomes reflected in the life of the believer.

Our text states that the Sun of Righteousness will have "healing in His wings." Sin brought death and destruction for the soul and body. But Christ brings healing for the disease of sin and restores health to the soul.

The final facet of this radiant textual jewel is that the delivered soul will cavort and skip like a calf that has been confined to the stall and is suddenly freed. This speaks of the exuberance of life imparted by the Sun of Righteousness.

The first promise God gave to Adam at the dawn of Creation (Gen. 3:15) was a feeble spark. But here, in the last book of prophecy, that spark was enlarged until it became the Sun of Righteousness who was to bring illumination to the whole world.

Pearls of the Prophets

The pearls of the prophets all lie loose and unstrung. These penmen of God saw things they did not understand, but in faith proclaimed them for generations to come. It would be 400 years after Malachi before the Sun of Righteousness would break forth. Then Christ, the Pearl of Greatest Price, would radiantly fulfill all that the prophets had said. Praise God!

God of the prophets, thank You for their radiant revelations and inspired insights that aid my understanding and enrich my soul.